Illustrated by QBN Studios

Contents

SAVE
THE ANIMALS
May the forest
be with you

Hello readers!

Hello readers! Today I will be interviewing five animals. Any guesses? No, I'm not interviewing a tiger, a bear, or even a whale. We'll get to that in a second.

These wonderful animals are special in a sad way. They have dwindled to the point that they are now considered critically endangered.

What did I say? I know! I know! Let me explain. Critically endangered means that there are not a lot of them. If we do not help them very soon, we will lose all of them forever! Yes, you and I could help keep them alive.

The animals in this book are not only critically endangered, they are neither as popular as deer, kangaroo, or sharks. So, they can easily experience societal extinction. Wait, I know what you are thinking: "what does societal extinction mean?"

Simply, we forget about them. Think of societal extinction like a toy you once had. Then, you lost your toy or it got stolen. A very long time has passed since then and now you don't even remember having the toy in the first place. You don't remember what it looked like or even how you used to play with it.

Let's save our Mother Earth
earth

Just like that, if we do not help these animals, they will completely disappear and we will forget that they ever lived on earth with us.

Imagine how these animals would feel if they could talk for themselves...

In this book, we will take an adventurous journey to get to know these beautiful animal friends a little better. They are going to share with us some important facts about themselves.

Learning about them is the best way to help them. Are you ready for a ride together? Hop in and make yourself comfy.

Let's go!

First in line, the Asian Unicorn

Oh! Hi there!

What do you see? Do you see a tail? That's me! My parents call me Bạnbè. Let me help you say it. Bun-Bei. Yes, I know, it is close to Bambi.

My name means 'friend' in Vietnamese.

You, humans, call me saola. My nickname is Asian Unicorn because we are very rare!

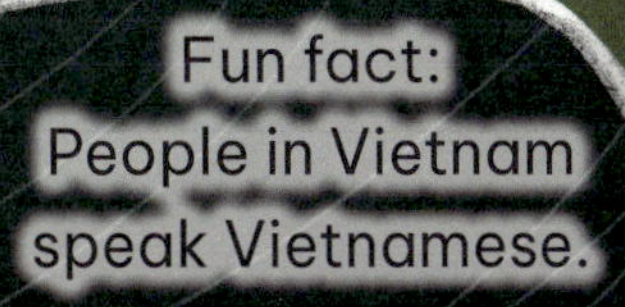

My Evergreen Home!

I'm walking through lush green forests, deep murky swamps, and big dark caves around me. It is wet, cool, and rainy most of the year here. It is fun to feel the cold breeze tickling my nose. I can feel tiny water drops patting my head.

I love to dance around with my little skinny legs; I love to feel the wet grass under my hooves. I only live in dense evergreen forests in the Annamite mountains on the border of Vietnam and Laos.

I am so happy to be free, deep in the forest! I feel lucky to be in my home!

Time for breakfast!

Today, we have leaves, fruits, seeds, and berries on the menu! There is a juicy berry. Gulp! Where is the berry? Oh, it is in my tummy. I did not notice it!

We eat only plants and do not eat meat. Another name for animals like us who eat only plants is herbivores.

What did you eat for breakfast? I am pretty sure you enjoyed it!

Num, num, num! HUH!

Oh-oh! I heard something. I got to gallop!!!

Phew! That was close!!!

There was a tiger on the loose!

Tigers, crocodiles, and humans are our predators.

Predators are animals that hunt or eat other animals. Like, cats eating mice.

I felt scared, and I was trembling. Mama and Papa always say, "lookout and be alert for anyone who wants to eat you. We use our strong horns to fight predators. We are really fast too and can outrun them, but not all the time."

Look into the pond

My friends and I enjoy playing in this big blue pond! Do you see my beautiful reflection on the water?

Humans say we look like antelopes. But we are different than them.

I can see the fascinating white markings on my face. Our fur is red, brown, or black. Also, I have large eyes. My tail is fluffy, brown at the top, beige in the middle, and black at the end.

Like my mama, I will be 220 pounds (close to 100 kilograms) and a little over 2 feet (around 60 centimeters) tall when I grow up.

Oh, my beautiful horns! My horns are not fully grown yet. Both my parents have humongous horns that curve backward.

It is not like any other animals' horns, neither like that of cows and giraffes; my horns sit parallel on my head.

Oh, but sadly, humans hunt us for our horns. They take them to sell at high prices or keep them as trophies!

I need your help!

We are losing our home because humans chop down trees and plants for wood and land. We struggle to survive because we get caught in snares that humans set up for other animals.

The worst thing is humans hunt us for our unique horns because they think it can be a beautiful display on their walls.

Our kind cannot survive in captivity.

So, only you can help us. Please preserve our habitat, and it will help us to stay alive.

Next up, it is the smallest porpoise in the world

Oh! How do you do?

Splash!!!

What is that sound? It's me! Would you like a tour around where we live?

Oh, I almost forgot to introduce myself! My name is Amiga, which means 'friend' in Spanish. I am a vaquita. Let me help you say it! Va-ki-ta.

Ready for the tour? On the count of three, 1, 2, 3! Let's go!

Fun fact: Spanish and its variations are spoken by many countries such as Spain, Mexico, Costa Rica, El Salvador, Guatemala, Honduras, Nicaragua, Panama, Cuba, Dominican Republic, Puerto Rico, Argentina, Bolivia, and Chile.

The sea waves back at me!

I swim, swim, and swim through forests of seaweed, deep, dark underwater caves, and lots of fish!

I feel waves brush past me! I glide through the water with as much elegance as a swan!

I jump up, do a full turn in mid-air, and take a breath of air before diving back into the water!

I feel fortunate to have a home sweet home— the Gulf of California in Mexico!

Do you want to join me for breakfast?

Today on the menu are fish, crustaceans, and squid! A scrumptious squid is waiting to be eaten! Gulp! Yummy, that sure is tasty! Gulp! Gulp! Gulp!

We eat both plants and meat, and that makes me an omnivore! Om-ni-vore.

We use echolocation to hunt for our food! Echolocation means calling out and listening to see how much time it takes for me to hear back my sound. It is our superpower!

Wait! I see a shadow, and it is coming my way! Sorry, but I gotta swim. See you on the next wave!

WOW! I have never seen a shark that big before!

That was close! It was a shark! I did not see that coming!

Sharks are our predators! They eat only meat. That makes them carnivores. Here, let me help you say it. Car-ni-vor.

Do I look good?

Our kind holds the title for the smallest porpoise in the world. When I grow up, I will be 4-5 feet (120 - 150 centimeters) in length and will weigh around 90 lbs (41 kilograms).

My body is round in shape with no noticeable beak. That gives me a clearly different look from my dolphin cousins.

Our body is grey, with darker skin along the top and lighter skin along our belly. I have a black outline of my mouth and eyes.

I need your help!

Do you know why I am endangered? No? Let me explain.

Long ago, we lived peaceful lives with nothing disturbing us besides the usual predators like sharks. Then, you humans started using gill-nets, which are long floating nets that trap fish. We get entangled in these nets and drown because we need to come to the surface to breathe but we cannot do that when we are all tangled up.

There are only a very few of us left alive today. We cannot survive in captivity, like in zoos or breeding centers.

You must be thinking, “that’s really bizarre!” And yes, it is! So, I am just politely asking, could you help us, please?

The Mexican government has made gill-nets illegal, but people still use them to catch totoaba fish, which are also endangered.

Please help us by using the correct ways to fish and not using gill nets.

Let's Meet the Owl Parrot

Nice to meet you!

What is that green puffball next to that bush? It's me! I am a kakapo. I know it sounds like catapult but say it with me, it is kuh-kaa-pow. I am also known as an owl parrot.

My name is Harioka. My name means happy in the Māori language. I am really friendly!

Would you like me to show you around? Yes? Then, let's go!

Fun fact: The native people in New Zealand speak the Māori language.

The trees sway in my way!

I jump and hop and wiggle my tail. It is fun to play in the breeze. I dance and turn around. I leap around. I jump, jump, and jump into the crisp air. I want to climb a tree. I grip onto the tree.

We only live in the rainforests of New Zealand, a place that is close to Australia. I feel lucky to have my green home.

Do you like to have lunch?

Oh, I looove lunch! Do you want to join me? Okay.

We eat fruits, seeds, leaf buds, shoots, tubers, rhizomes, pollen, mosses, and fungi. My favorite one is Rimu fruit. In fact, I see one right now. Gulp! I feel it slide down my throat and into my awaiting belly.

I'm gonna enjoy these Rimu fruits. See you on the next page.

I think I am a pretty bird!

When I grow up, I will be around 9 pounds or 4 kilograms (Oh, that is heavy!). I have a face of an owl, I stand like a penguin, and walk like a duck. Pretty neat, right?

I am brown and green. I like to climb trees using my long and sharp claws that help me to grip the tree.

I'm a solitary bird. That means I enjoy living by myself.

You know, we are the heaviest parrots in the world. Also, we are the only flightless parrots in the world. Flightless means I can't fly, like a kiwi bird or an ostrich.

Scientists do not know how long we live. But they think that we live 40-80 years!

My home is my sanctuary!

We don't live on the mainland of New Zealand. That's because there are a lot of our predators, such as cats, stoats, mice, and rats. All of these were introduced to New Zealand by you humans.

Now, because we are the heaviest parrot in the world and can't fly, our only way to escape is to run from these predators. But usually, the predators can run faster than us and catch us. Rats and mice also raid our nests and eat the eggs.

Now, our population only lives on the three islands where there are no predators to threaten us. Those are Codfish Island, Little Barrier Island, and Anchor Island.

I feel safe every day because now I live in a predator-free island.

I need your help!

We are critically endangered! We are almost extinct!

It was not like this before. Long ago, we happily walked around the main island with no predators to scare us. When people discovered New Zealand, they cleared out our habitat and introduced predators.

Now, the New Zealand government is helping us by removing the animals that can hunt us.
If you help us by controlling our predators and creating safe spaces, we will be back to our usual life!

Jump in to know about a bright amphibian

Whoosh, glide, and glide!!!

Oh, there you are! I didn't know you were here!

My name is Oumarou. I'll show you how to say it: Oo-mah-roo.

I'm a tadpole, and I will grow up to be a red-bellied egg frog.

Do you want me to show you around? Okay! Then let's go!

What a wonderful stream!

I glide through the fresh, clear water in the valley of Mt. Manengouba in Cameroon, Africa. In the stream, my favorite places are pools.

My tail steers me through the water like a platypus. Swishing my tail back and forth behind me is my favorite style.

I've just started to grow back legs!

When I grow into a frog, I will use my long and strong legs to jump and hop into other places, such as gravel banks, roots, dense undergrowth, and swim in streams.

Fun fact: I am an amphibian. You know, amphibians are frogs, toads, and salamanders. We are special; we use gills to breathe when we are young and live underwater. Then, we grow up and develop lungs to be able to breathe and live on land.

Do I look good?

Do you wonder why humans call me the Red-bellied-egg frog? It is because of my belly color, which will be completely red when I grow up. The female frogs, like my mama, are bigger than males. Males are darker than females.

I have to go through a huge process called a life cycle: yes, it is like a circle. First, my momma lays her eggs, and I hatch out as a tadpole.

In the beginning, I only live in the water and use gills for breathing, just like a fish.

Next, I grow more: first, my back legs, then my front legs form. As my tail goes away, I become an adult frog and use my lungs for breathing.

Finally, I hop out of the water. Tik, tik, tik, and the cycle starts again.

Breakfast is ready!

Momma and Papa never tell me what they, frogs, eat, but I think it is delicious.
Now, because I'm a tadpole, my daily food is algae.
There is a big patch of algae that looks scrumptious.
Slurp slurp.

Mmm, mmm, good! It feels wonderful as it slides down my throat and into my belly!

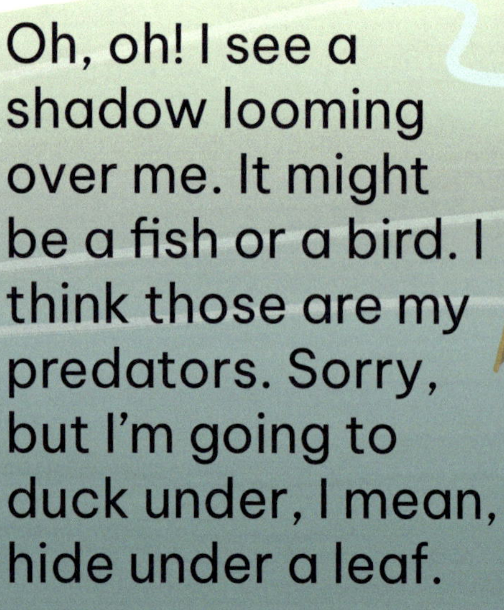

Oh, oh! I see a shadow looming over me. It might be a fish or a bird. I think those are my predators. Sorry, but I'm going to duck under, I mean, hide under a leaf.

I need your help!

It was a long day. But let's wrap it up by saying why I need your help.

We are endangered! Our only home is the mountain slopes of Mt. Manengouba.

Humans are clearing the forests and the streams where we breed and live. They use our spaces to make buildings. Also, when the forests along the streams are cleared, the clear, clean water becomes muddy and brown, which is not good for us to survive. Isn't that sad?

So, I'm asking y'all: can YOU help us please, by leaving the trees and streams as they naturally are?

Oh, hello!

Zzzzzz, fish, fish, fish. Zzzzzz, fish, fish, fish.

Huh? What happened? Oh, I know, I was dreaming about eating fish.

I am a gharial. Ha ha, no, not gorilla, silly. Ga-ri-yal. Want to see the murky waters? Yes? Then let's go!

Wait, a second, I forgot to introduce myself! My name is Yara.

Do you know what my name means? It means 'friend' in the Hindi language. My momma tells me that we are the only friendly crocodilian species. It is lovely to be friends with everyone.

Fun fact: Hindi is a language in India.

Finally, it is the friendly fish-eating crocodile

We gharials are special.

Humans say our ancestors lived with dinosaurs. Think about that! I am proud of my great-grandparents.

- In epee standard foil parries are used, along with the **CIRCULAR 6TH** parry, in which the blade executes a teardrop movement returning a disengage to the inside of the arm to its starting point on the outside. Note that Circular 6th is not circular; a true circle allows the opponent's blade to slip out of the parry.

- In sabre beginners are commonly taught three parries:

    - **3RD** - a high outside parry
    - **4TH** - a high inside parry
    - **5TH** - a parry that defends the head from vertical cuts

- **DISTANCE CONTROL** – generally by a rapid short retreat to move the target sufficiently back so the attack falls short.

- **EVASIONS** – any movement of the body designed to avoid being touched, such as a ducking or sidestepping.

Counteroffense

Counter offensive actions are counter-attacks – an attack into an opponent's attack without any attempt to parry. The most commonly taught one is the **STOP HIT** or **STOP CUT** (in sabre), a simple direct movement to hit the opponent's target as quickly as possible.

Footwork

Footwork is a key component of modern fencing, certainly as important as bladework, and possibly even more important. Footwork maintains the distance, allows the fencer to close the distance when attacking, and carries the attack to target. These actions may be executed from:

- The **ON GUARD** position – the basic static position from which all actions flow.

- **ADVANCE** – a step forward.

- **RETREAT** – a step backward.

- **LUNGE** – a forward extension of the body led by a kick and driven by the rear leg.

- **RETREAT-LUNGE** – a retreat followed immediately by a lunge.

- **ADVANCE-LUNGE** – an advance followed immediately by a lunge.

In addition, four other advanced footwork movements may be used, although they are not normally taught to beginners. The use of the forward pass and the fleche is prohibited in sabre.

- **FORWARD PASS** – a movement in which the rear foot crosses the front foot going forward, and then the front foot crosses the rear to establish the original on-guard position.

- **BACKWARDS PASS** – the reverse of the forward pass in which the front foot passes the rear foot going backwards, and then the rear foot crosses to return to the original on guard position.

- **BALESTRA** - a combination of forward jump and lunge.

- **FLECHE** or **FLUNGE** - an explosive running (foil and epee) or jumping (sabre) movement.

13. How Do Athletes Learn?

Individuals learn physical skills in a variety of ways. The challenge to you as an instructor is to find an approach that engages the way in which a particular athlete learns, and then use that approach effectively.

Although there are differences in the names used to describe these learning styles, and even differences in the styles included, the set that seems to make the most sense for us as fencing coaches is:

VISUAL – learn by seeing demonstrations of technique, are sensitive to body language, and often wish to stand where they can best see the movement.

AUDITORY – learn by hearing, are sensitive to tone and pitch of voice, and benefit from repeating back instructions you have given them.

KINESTHETIC – learn by practicing the technique and feeling the movement, are sensitive to descriptions of how an action feels and to being placed in correct positions.

SEQUENTIAL – learn by analyzing and building a logical order between linear steps in an action, engage when you ask them why and when to do the skill.

Individuals may learn in more than one way, with one style being dominant. As a result the more of these characteristic styles you engage in teaching, the more likely you are to succeed with the individual and the more likely you are to reach students in a group lesson. This suggests that the basic flow of any instruction is:

- **Tell** the fencers what you are going to teach them, where it fits, and why it is important – engages auditory and sequential learners.

- **Demonstrate** the skill, breaking down its parts – engages visual and sequential learners.

- Have the fencers **perform** the technique with corrections – engages the auditory, visual, and kinesthetic learners.

- **Review** the technique (both telling and demonstrating) and its components – engages all learning styles.

The **TELL-DEMONSTRATE-PERFORM-REVIEW** model is a core approach to teaching and training your athletes, and should be something you do automatically.

Regardless of the style used, one constant is **REPETITION**. Fencers have to execute a skill multiple times before they can reliably do so in competition. Some instructors in the martial arts use the figure of 10,000 repetitions before a skill is mastered; others cite 50,000. Regardless of which number is correct, repetition is essential. Constantly reviewing techniques already taught has the benefit of giving your students opportunities to build toward the number of repetitions needed.

Review also serves another purpose. One of the key principles of training is **RECENCY** – we remember best that which we have done most recently. A technique not practiced may gradually decay. Even well executed techniques that are part of a fencer's favorite repertoire for competition require regular review and practice.

This means that there are essentially two key activities in developing a fencer: teaching and training. **TEACHING** focuses on the communication of how and when to execute a technique, and **TRAINING** focuses on building the fencer's ability to execute under combat conditions in the bout and tournament.

14. Teaching Basic Skills

Assistant Moniteurs should be prepared to teach basic skills that are appropriate for students in a beginning fencing course. If we teach skills, we have a responsibility to teach our students effective means of executing fencing actions. Teaching your athletes correct technique is a basic ethical responsibility that you assume when you decide that you are going to be a coach.

How we execute techniques as competitors is not necessarily how we should teach students. Every experienced fencer has individual approaches to performing fencing skills, approaches that work for the fencer, but may not work for other fencers. The new fencer, especially, should be taught standard ways of performing skills.

What Is A Basic Skill?

Basic skills are techniques that form the core building blocks of fencing a specific weapon. Advanced skills are formed by using basic skills as their foundation and either adding other basic skills, developing a skill to an advanced state, or adding new, more technically difficult skills to solve problems that the basic skill cannot solve.

As an example, advance, retreat, and lunge are basic core footwork skills. The advance-lunge, a combination of two basic skills, has become a basic skill itself because of rules changes and the increased athleticism of the sport. The forward and backwards passes are actually old basic skills, deeply embedded in Medieval longsword technique, that reemerged to solve the problem of covering larger amounts of ground without having to do multiple advances and retreats. The fleche developed initially as a combination of forward pass into lunge to deal with opponents with very fast footwork, and eventually morphed into the flunge for sabre fencers to circumvent rules changes that eliminated the fleche.

Trends in Teaching These Skills

Over the past 20 years there has been a significant change in how we teach students. These changes have improved the teaching and training of athletes. Five major themes now describe how we teach and train:

Realism. What you teach must be what students will encounter in competition. Every action you take as a coach in the lesson must be realistic and calculated to simulate bout conditions as accurately as possible. Introducing unrealistic elements will train the fencer to react inappropriately, to make incorrect tactical choices, and to fail to recognize actual opportunities to score or defend successfully. Your students will fight the way you have trained them.

This extends to what fencers will do with their partners in practice. In drills, you must ensure that fencers work their training partners realistically, not serve up puff balls for easy and relaxed response to simulate a drill. Left alone, many beginning fencers or fencers who do not regularly compete will adjust their speed, distance, and movement patterns to allow their partner to complete the drill with as little chance of failure (and as little effort) as possible. This cheats both participants, the attacker because he or she is not developing a quality attack, and the defender because he or she is not developing the ability to actually defend.

Cues. A **CUE** is some action or failure to act by the coach that causes the student to execute a technique or tactic. The key question for the coach is "what will cause my fencer to execute the desired action?"

This is a complicated issue in coaching because the cue must be something the student can recognize, but it must also be realistic. Every cue must be something that an opponent would actually do on the strip. Otherwise you are teaching your students to recognize and react to something they will not see in competition, and, by omission, not teaching them to recognize actual opportunities. Many cues routinely used are not realistic – for example, raising a hand when we want the fencer to lunge in a footwork drill. If you have ever seen an opponent do that in a bout, please post the video on You-Tube so we can all enjoy it.

Therefore cues used in teaching must be scaled to the ability of the student, be clear, and not overload the student. Good cues prepare the student for competition by accurately simulating bout conditions.

- Beginner level cues. In general, cues in working with beginners should be slower and larger than you would use for a more advanced fencer. They must be unambiguous, so that the fencer will choose the correct action. Avoid swamping the fencer with multiple cues, especially potentially contradictory ones. Most work that Assistant Moniteurs will do will require the ability to do this level of cuing.

- Tactical level cues. Cues in some exercises for advanced intermediates and higher level fencers should be more tactical in nature. Now you can use a combination of footwork, distance, blade cues, and the situation on the tactical wheel to provide the stimulus for student action. As control transitions to the student, the student can use cues to draw the reaction from you that they need to complete the action.

Teaching cues in a drill situation is challenging in that the students have to learn how to execute the skill and how to execute the cue. The benefit is that when you teach a cue you are teaching the fencer how to trigger a specific action predictably – you are teaching the **INVITATION** for each action. Two examples of how this might work:

- A simple blade cue in foil:

  Step 1 - Fencer A moves his blade to the inside opening the line of 6th
  Step 2 – as he does so Fencer B executes a straight thrust with lunge to hit in 6th as it opens

  Fencer A has executed an invitation, and has learned how much of an invitation is needed to draw an attack. Fencer B has seen an opening as it develops and attacked into the opening line, practicing the straight thrust.

  The hidden message is that Fencer A now knows how to stimulate Fencer B to lunge into 6th. This sets up the next step:

  Step 3 – Fencer A executes a 6th parry, and ripostes to hit Fencer B as she attacks.

- A more complicated cue in any weapon using blade and footwork:

  Step 1 – Fencer A alternates advancing in a good guard position and retreating either in a good guard or with her blade lowered.
  Step 2 – Fencer B maintains distance
  Step 3 – Fencer A advances with a lowered blade
  Step 4 – Fencer B attacks.

Tactics. Every technique should be taught in the context of its tactical application. Techniques do not exist in a vacuum. They are part of the flow of the bout, and should be taught in the framework of where and when they can be used logically.

Techniques are specific actions or skills used in the bout – a disengage is a technique. Techniques are relatively stable in the bout, although they may require minor modification to deal with a particular opponent. However, tactics are the choice of a combination of techniques, timing, distance, initiative, preparation, speed, and psychology to solve the problem of hitting the opponent in a bout. Tactics are set by your plan for the bout and constantly reevaluated and modified as conditions change.

There are a variety of approaches to understanding tactics, including wheels, trees, and grids. The tactical model you will need to be able to work with is the Short Tactical Wheel – a way of thinking about how to shift tactics to deal with the opponent's actions.

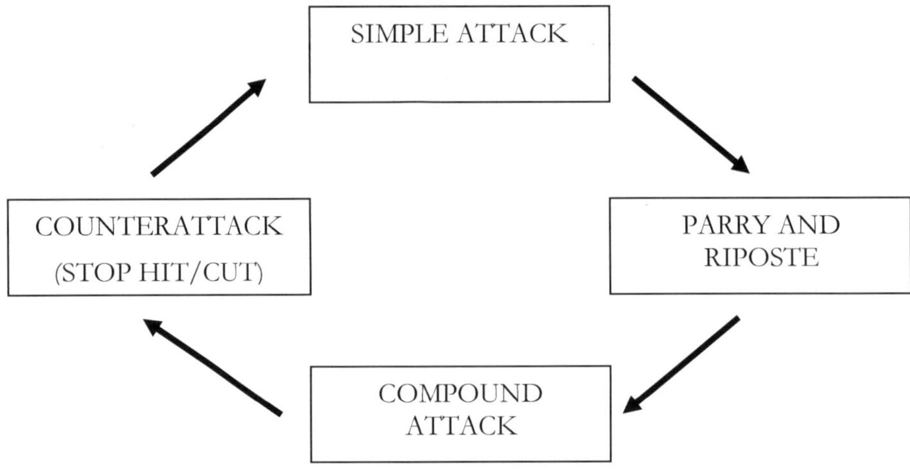

Figure 1. The Short Tactical Wheel

Fencer A starts the bout, and absent any other information, attacks with a simple attack. When Fencer A executes a simple attack, Fencer B should parry and riposte to defeat the attack. Fencer A, when expecting to be parried, should execute a compound attack to deceive the parry. Fencer B then counterattacks the compound attack with a stop hit. In turn Fencer A defeats the stop hit with a simple attack.

Although the tactical wheel appears orderly, it is really fuzzy. Depending on the opponent you can start at various places. In sabre and epee the stop hit may be a reasonable counteroffensive answer to simple attacks. And compound attack is too limiting; it is really any attack that uses a first action to prepare for the final.

This is also a tool for predicting what an opponent may do. If Fencer A knows that Fencer B expects a simple attack and will be ready to parry it, then Fencer A should execute a compound attack to defeat the parry. However, Fencer B understands that Fencer A expects a parry and will do a compound action, and therefore Fencer B executes an immediate stop hit when Fencer A starts to move. This is the Iocaine Powder problem (a specific approach to tactics) from the movie *The Princess Bride*, a fencers' cult classic.

Do not teach the tactical wheel as "you change when it does not work." Changing when something doesn't work is likely to mean you changes when you were hit. Change when it is clear the opponent understands what is happening, and is ready to counter it.

From the perspective of teaching, this means that you as the coach must:

- Introduce tactics as early as possible in a fencer's development. One way to do this is to teach using the tactical wheel. For example, if you teach a simple attack, teach the answering parry and riposte combination.

- Remember that every action potentially serves as a feint for the next action. Have students build on their last action. For example, if an attack in 6th worked, then execute the next attack by feint of straight thrust into 6th-disengage to hit in 4th.

- Drill students until they can make tactical transitions quickly. A change in the opponent's actions should trigger an immediate reevaluation and adjustment by the fencer.

Tempo. In modern fencing distance, timing, and initiative are core elements of scoring hits. Tempo is a key part of the timing element, and should be taught at the first opportunity. For beginning and early intermediate students, this introduction can start with varying the speed of actions.

For footwork, design footwork exercises that cause the student to vary the speed of advances, retreats, and lunges. For example:

- If you have the fencers practice footwork by advancing or retreating the length of a strip, have them do various zones of the strip at different speeds.

- If you do instructor led footwork, vary your speed of movement, at first predictably, and then increasingly unpredictably.

- When they do footwork drills with a partner, have the fencer controlling the drill vary the speed of movement.

- When they do lunges, have them vary the speed of the lunge, first in order and then randomly through slow, medium, and fast to accelerating from a slow start to a fast finish.

For bladework, have the students similarly vary their speed of action. For example:

- Have them execute simple attacks slowly, at medium speed, fast, and with a slow start to a fast finish.

- Have them execute parries at one speed and ripostes at a faster speed.

- Have them execute compound attacks with a slow feint, followed by a fast final action.

At this level the goal is to develop the capability to recognize different speeds, execute at those different speeds, and to do so consciously.

Transition to Student Control of the Action. Fencing lessons traditionally are coach driven. The coach presents the cues, controls the direction of movement, etc., and the student reacts to the coach's actions. The problem with this is that we want the fencer to then be able to fence a bout in which he or she seizes the initiative and drives the actions. For the fencer to learn how to take the initiative and control the action, we have to find ways to shift control from the coach to students as early as possible.

Areas in which you can shift control relatively easily as students develop include the following:

- Footwork. Traditionally the coach leads with footwork. In at least part of the lesson you could have the student initiate the footwork, with you following his or her lead.

This is more difficult for the coach, as you have to anticipate when to create openings based on the student's movement.

- When to attack. Allow the student to choose when to attack, with the expectation that they will not attack on every cue you present. The focus should be on the student attacking when conditions are right for the student.

- Who initiates the action. This is a complicated concept. When we open a line and step forward, we expect the student to attack with a straight thrust or cut. But the student does not initiate the action, we do (our opening the line and stepping forward is the controlling initiation). So we are teaching the student not to dominate the action and create conditions, but rather to react to conditions the opponent creates for them. And always reacting is not the way to win bouts. Therefore it is important to find ways to allow the student to initiate the action. Allowing student control of both footwork and when to attack can be combined with allowing student decision as to which technique to employ to create a more realistic environment. For example:

    - control of footwork - student advances and retreats with coach moving in reaction with some variation in the length of steps the coach takes.

    - when to attack – student initiates attack when the student believes conditions are favorable to hit.

    - choice of attack – the coach maintains a partially open line in 6th and the student executes a straight thrust with opposition or a disengage.

At the intermediate level more options for student control and initiation exist, and training will be better understood and more tactically useful to the student. However, look for ways to start the process of developing student initiative as early as you can. There is a good discussion of ways to do this with even beginner level footwork in the footwork section of the group lesson in the Group Lesson Mechanics section of this book.

Actions, Cues, and Applications

As an Assistant Moniteur, your students will observe how you execute techniques and model their performance on your actions, especially when you do not intend for them to do so, and especially with techniques that they are not prepared to execute correctly. All of us have idiosyncratic techniques that work for us, but that are not generally translatable to our students. Teach and model core technique, not your individual variants, and not what you saw a world champion do in a video. As they develop, students will find variations of technique that work for them, but they cannot do that in a rational way if they are not first taught the core technique.

The following tables describe the key elements of the fencing techniques that you should be able to perform flawlessly and teach well at the Assistant Moniteur level, and provide cues that you can use to lead students to execute the techniques.

Table 1. Core Element of Assistant Moniteur Level Skills

Action	Core Elements
Grip	For either French or pistol grip in foil or epee: • Index finger under the handle with the handle resting on the middle segment • Thumb on top of the grip over the index finger • Other 3 fingers relaxed and controlling the shaft of the French grip or the hooks of the pistol grip • Handle is oriented in the longitudinal grove of the hand • Blade is in a straight line from tip to hand to elbow For the standard sabre grip: • Handle held vertically to 45 degrees forward of vertical in the vertical groove of the hand, <u>not</u> against the meat of thumb in a grip similar to foil • Thumb on the back of the grip, pointing in the direction of the cutting edge • Hand may be close to the bell or closer to the pommel, based on how you teach use of the blade
Attention	• Feet at 90 degree angle on the fencing line • Torso is upright, and head faces the opponent • Weapon arm is toward the opponent with the blade extending in front • Rear arm hangs freely at the side
Salute	• From attention • Blade is brought smoothly up so that the guard is at mouth level • And then lowered smartly
On Guard	• Feet at 90 degree angle on the fencing line and approximately shoulder width apart • Torso is upright, sitting at approximately 45 degrees across the hips, and the head faces the opponent • Weapon arm is toward the opponent raised approximately 10-15 degrees above the horizontal in foil with the blade extending in front so that its point is even with the opponent's shoulder. In epee and sabre the arm is parallel to the ground. • Elbow is tucked in, wrist is slightly displaced outward, weapon point is directed with the opponent's torso • Rear arm is bent at shoulder height behind the torso, with the forearm vertical and the hand relaxed in foil and epee. In sabre the fencer's fist sits on the rear hip. *Note – many if not almost all experienced fencers fence with the non-weapon arm and hand in a much lower position. The position described is the classic position; we advocate its use with beginners to teach head up, level shoulders, and maximum reach on the extension as the arm falls in the lunge. Once fencers have experience they may be allowed to develop a body position that best fits their and their coach's style.*

<table>
<tr><td>Advance</td><td>Note – this description is of the quick step advance.
• Movement is in legs, torso and head remain upright and stable
• Front leg swings forward, landing on the heel
• Rear leg comes forward reestablishing the normal distance between the feet
• Front foot and rear foot land at the same time</td></tr>
<tr><td>Retreat</td><td>• Movement is in legs, torso and head remain upright and stable
• Rear leg swings backward, reaching with the toe
• Front leg moves backward reestablishing the normal distance between the feet
• Front foot and rear foot land at the same time</td></tr>
<tr><td>Lunge</td><td>• Extension of the weapon arm starts the lunge
• As the arm reaches approximately one half to two thirds extension, the front foot kicks forward
• The rear leg simultaneously drives the body forward
• As the arm completes the extension
• The rear arm drops to the rear
• And the hit lands just before the front foot lands
• Recovery is by all limbs bending simultaneously to return rearward or forward to the guard position</td></tr>
<tr><td>Advance-Lunge</td><td>• Depending on the weapon and the tactical situation, the arm extension may start before the initiation of the advance or before initiation of the lunge
• An accelerating quick step advance
• As soon as both feet have landed in the quick step, the lunge initiates without hesitation</td></tr>
<tr><td>Straight Thrust</td><td>• Point is lowered, with fingers controlling the motion of the point
• Arm extends smoothly to full extension
• In general, arm is at shoulder height (or slightly above in epee)
• Extension is direct to target or maintaining a closed line, depending on the situation</td></tr>
<tr><td>Direct Cut (sabre)</td><td>• Arm extends smoothly to full extension with the blade at an angle of 135 degrees or greater.
• In general, arm is at shoulder height
• Extension is direct to target or maintaining a closed line in opposition (only in 3rd), depending on the situation
• Cut is delivered with finger action as blade reaches target</td></tr>
<tr><td>Disengage</td><td>• Point is lowered, with fingers controlling the motion of the point
• Point passes around the opponent's guard from one line to another
• Simultaneously the arm starts to extend so that the movement is steadily progressive toward the target
• As the arm moves into the final line of attack, any needed footwork carries the blade forward to the target as the extension is completed</td></tr>
<tr><td>Change of engagement</td><td>• Point is lowered, with fingers controlling the motion of the point
• Point passes around the opponent's guard from one line to another
• As the blade rises to engagement, the forearm and wrist move to close the new line of engagement</td></tr>
</table>

Counterdisengage	• On the opponent's change of engagement or circular attempt to take the blade • The point follows the opponent's movement in a circle to return to the original line • Simultaneously the arm starts to extend so that the movement is steadily progressive toward the target • As the arm moves into the final line of attack, any needed footwork carries the blade forward to the target as the extension is completed
Coupe (sabre)	• Point is raised, with fingers controlling the motion of the point • Point passes around the tip of the opponent's blade from one line to another • Simultaneously the arm starts to extend so that the movement is steadily progressive toward the target • As the arm moves into the final line of attack, any needed footwork carries the blade forward to the target as the extension is completed and the cut delivered with the fingers
Note to Parries	*Parries may be made with opposition (critical to controlling the opponent's blade in epee and opposition cuts in sabre) or by percussion. There are a wide variety of methods of completing the parry. The following description is general and covers the arm, hand, and blade position at completion.*
Parry 3 (sabre)	• The arm is parallel to the fencing line to the outside of the fencer's thigh or offset to the outside of this position, based on the force of the attack • The wrist turns the guard to the outside to protect the arm and displace the opponent's blade • Elbow in, wrist out, blade parallel to the fencing line but in a position to threaten the opponent's target
Parry 4 (foil and sabre)	• The arm swings across the fencer's target to position the guard and blade so that the inside line is closed. • In sabre, the guard should be in line with the forearm, blade up • In foil the blade is parallel to the fencing line but with the point in a position to threaten the opponent's target
Parry 5 (sabre)	• Hand is raised to head height, slightly to the outside of the fencing line • Blade is angled forward and across the body with the point just above the level of the guard • Elbow in, wrist out • Parry should be forward of the torso, not over the head
Parry 6 (foil and epee)	• The arm is parallel to the fencing line to the outside of the fencer's thigh • Elbow in, wrist out, blade parallel to the fencing line but with the point in a position to threaten the opponent's target.
Parry Circular 6 (epee)	• On the opponent's disengage • The point follows the opponent's movement in a circle to return to the original line • The arm is parallel to the fencing line to the outside of the fencer's

	thigh • Elbow in, wrist out, blade parallel to the fencing line but with the point in a position to threaten the opponent's target
Direct Riposte	• Executed immediately on completion of the parry • Moves by the most direct movement to the target with the blade moving rapidly into the attacking position • Finger control is used to make point placement (foil and epee) or to direct the cut (sabre). • Is either static or done with an advance or a lunge as needed.

Table 2. Cues for Assistant Moniteur Level Techniques

Action	Cue	Phase of Tactical Wheel
Attention	• Start or end of bout • Start or end of lesson	
Salute	• Start or end of bout • Start or end of lesson	
On Guard	• Referee command	
Advance	• Distance is long distance or beyond • Opponent retreats	
Retreat	• Distance is such that opponent can hit • Opponent advances	
Lunge	• Distance is medium – opponent has open line – timing is correct for attack	Simple attack
Advance Lunge	• Opponent starts to step back on start of extension of the arm	Simple attack
Straight Thrust	• Opening of a line, horizontally or vertically – distance and timing correct for attack	Simple attack
Direct Cuts (sabre)	• Opening of a line, horizontally or vertically – distance and timing correct for attack	Simple attack
Disengage	• Pressure on the blade • Sweep attempting to take the blade • Current line closed - distance and timing correct for attack	Simple attack
Change of engagement	• Opponent change of engagement • Line closed	Preparation for a simple attack
Counterdisengage	• Opponent change of engagement or circular taking – distance and timing correct for attack	Simple attack
Coupe (sabre)	• Pressure on the blade • Sweep attempting to take the blade • Current line closed - distance and timing correct for attack	Simple attack
Parry 3 (sabre)	• Attack into the outside line	Parry and riposte

Parry 4 (foil and sabre)	• Attack into the inside line	Parry and riposte
Parry 5 (sabre)	• Vertical attack to the head	Parry and riposte
Parry 6 (foil and epee)	• Attack into the outside line	Parry and riposte
Parry Circular 6 (epee)	• Attack from 6th to 4th by disengage	Parry and riposte
Direct Riposte	• Parried attack and open line	Parry and riposte

15. Demonstrating Skills

Demonstration is a key teaching skill – we expect our students to be able to perform what we demonstrate through practice and repetition.

Demonstration-performance is a standard approach to teaching a wide variety of physical skills, including sports skills. It is the core of the Tell-Demonstrate-Perform-Review model of teaching athletic skills. The demonstration-performance method consists of two central elements, the demonstration by the coach and a training partner, and subsequent performance by the students.

Demonstration engages the visual learner (remember that not all people learn best visually), supported as needed by oral instruction (to engage auditory learners). Remember, however to keep explanations brief and focused on the skill and its application.

Key Concepts

Based on how athletes learn and many years of experience by fencing masters, we can define a number of key concepts for successful demonstration.

- Known to unknown. Start with what the students already know and add the new elements to it. Remind the students that they do know parts of the skill, as the tendency may be to view new skills as all new, different, challenging, when in fact they are just built up from old skills. For example, a compound attack is two simple attacks the students already know, the first executed as a feint.

- Simple to complex. Start with the simplest element and add to it to make the more complex one. Students will have a better chance of understanding a skill if it can be broken into simpler elements. Even a straight thrust can be broken down into simpler elements.

- Slow to fast. Avoid the temptation to show your students how great you are by doing everything at the fastest possible speed. They may not see any part of what you do. Slow actions down to a crawl so the student can see the details.

- Students have to be able to see what you are doing. The student four ranks back in a mass class has no chance of seeing the action, much less the fine details of an action. Have the students move to where they can see. In some cases that may be glued to your shoulder or to your partner's shoulder. That may require encouragement as students become accustomed to their place in a class, and really do not like to invade what they perceive as your personal space to get a better look at the movement.

- Must be realistic. Your demonstrations must show a technique in the context of modern fencing. If you fence at a high level or coach at a high level you have a tremendous advantage in seeing what elite level fencers are doing. If you don't, and most Assistant Moniteurs do not, watch every bit of competition video you can find. Go to nearby North American Cup Circuit, Region Open Competitions, Super Youth Circuit, and other events that draw higher classification fencers and the best referees, and spend the day watching and taking notes. Understand what high level fencers are doing and how the referees call the action.

General Structure of a Demonstration

In a demonstration you want to engage as many different learning styles as possible. The successful demonstration does the Tell and Demonstrate parts of the Tell-Demonstrate-Perform-Review training cycle. The following basic procedure is applicable to individual lessons, small groups, and larger classes.

- Position yourself so the students can clearly see the important features of the action you are demonstrating.

- Name the skill. Fencing techniques often have more than one name. Pick a name that is commonly accepted and is methodologically correct and use it consistently. Tell the students what the skill is: "I am going to demonstrate a disengage."

- Provide the when and why of the skill, applicable to the context in which you are teaching it. For example, with the first explanation of the disengage to a beginner class: "we do the disengage when the opponent presses on our blade so that we can hit him in the opening line." A long description is not necessary, just enough information so that the students understand this is something useful.

- Demonstrate at reasonable speed. Show the skill fast enough for the students to understand its speed, but not so fast they cannot see it.

- Demonstrate the skill at a slower speed at which the students can easily see what is happening in the movement.

- Show each key part separately, in the order in which they are executed. For example, in the disengage from 6 to 4: (1) start of forward movement and lowering of the point, (2) pass the point around under the guard as the extension continues, and (3) with the rise into 4, lunge landing with the point before the front foot.

- Build up the parts – where logical, combine parts together into chunks in complex actions. There is evidence that short term memory is limited in the number of discrete items it can retain. By chunking items together we reduce the number of parts to remember and increase the probability the technique will transition to long term memory.

- Then demonstrate the whole action at a slow speed, so that the students can see the parts flow together.

- Finally demonstrate the entire skill at the same reasonably fast speed with which you started the demonstration.

- Be prepared to do it again, either parts or the whole demonstration. Students will look at you, nod, and say they have it, and not have a clue. One honest soul will say "could you do that again?" Welcome the chance.

A note on demonstration partners. Try to rotate among the students to pick someone to be your partner – this avoids the impression of favoritism. However, pick someone that you have confidence can perform their role. Some students may lack the skill level needed for a particular demonstration. And at least one student in every class will want to try to show you up by hitting you or parrying or … to prove how cool he or she is. A quiet corrective conversation off to the side about why they want to sabotage the other student's learning and whether or not they want to continue in the class will normally solve the problem.

Large Group Demonstrations

Demonstrating in the larger group lesson is similar to the process described above, but several factors become more important.

- Importance of visibility. In larger groups the ability of all the fencers to see the demonstration becomes a major problem. Do not hesitate to have the students break ranks and move to where they can see you.

- Demonstrations are inherently general in nature. They do not address the specific learning needs of individual students. As a result, the larger the class, the more time will be consumed in corrective action for beginning and intermediate groups.

- Aim for a common denominator. Your goal is to have most of the students understand the demonstration. Someone will not, no matter how hard you try, or how long you take. Solve these outliers with individual corrective demonstrations or corrective lessons.

- Take the time necessary – but not too much (be guided by less talking – more doing). The tendency is to tell the students everything you know about the subject. Tell them what they need to know to meet the lesson objectives.

Corrective Demonstrations

Corrective demonstration is a subset of the normal demonstration used in drills or during supervised bouting. The intent is to intervene and correct an observed problem (1) the student does not correct after a number of trials and (2) that will cause a performance problem.

- These demonstrations are one-on-one or one-on-two, instructor to student. One-on-one deals with one student's performance. Typically one-on-two is a solution when training partners misunderstand the drill or how the technique will be used in the drill.

- Be quick and focused on the specific problem. Every student has a number of possible problems for correction. Stay on the track of the skill you are teaching, and do not get sucked into fixing multiple problems.

- Find a position that allows the student to understand the correction. You may need to be in front of the student or on either side, and you may need to face toward or away from the student.

- Consider using guided performance. In guided performance, you use your hands to place the student in the correct starting position and to guide the student's motion through the correct trajectory. Your movement in guiding the body should be slow and smooth, ending in the correct position. Because this requires that you touch the student, you must make certain the student is comfortable with level of contact. If not you can use your weapon to help guide movement along with your hand on their weapon. It is a good idea to warn the student that your guiding will not feel exactly the same as their correct execution of the skill, because their muscles and joints are not doing the work.

Go back to a shortened group demonstration if there is a common theme to performance problems, with several fencers showing the same, or closely related, incorrect performances.

16. Group Lesson Mechanics

Group lessons are the most efficient way to teach a number of students. They allow you to teach a skill once, as opposed to a dozen times in individual lessons. They provide the students more fencers as practice partners. They build group cohesion and loyalty. And, from an economic standpoint, they maximize revenue per teaching hour. As a result the group lesson is the basis of most beginner and intermediate lessons, and forms the basis for team practice sessions for competitive fencers.

In this handbook we focus on the lesson Moniteurs have to be prepared to teach as a model for two reasons. First, it provides a well-structured approach to the group lesson. Second, this is a lesson format commonly used by professional coaches, and therefore one in which you can expect to be assigned to help teach. And finally, when you test for Moniteur, this is the lesson you will have to be able to teach. As a result we want you to start practicing toward that goal now.

Introduction

Although the Moniteur lesson does not include a formal introduction, doing a short introduction to each lesson is very important. This helps the students focus on the subject of the lesson, reminds them of what they have done in the previous lesson, and introduces how the lesson integrates with what they already know. The introduction should be short and to the point, not more than 3 sentences:

- A restatement of what they learned in the previous lesson.
- The subject of this lesson.
- How this lesson fits with the previous lesson, or if it does not, how it will build their skill set.

When the fencers step onto the practice area, it is a good practice to start activity with a formal group salute. I also recommend ending the lesson with a salute. This helps to make the salute an automatic focusing activity the fencer performs every time he or she is going to fence, and reinforces its automatic performance in competition.

Warm-Up

The warm-up includes exercises, games, stretching, etc. to increase physical and psychological readiness for fencing. The closer warm-up activities come to movement patterns that will be used in fencing, the more effective they are in preparing the athlete.

- The warm-up should not be an extended activity. Current research shows that long warm-ups fatigue the athlete and actually reduce readiness. In most fencing settings approximately 10-15 minutes is sufficient. If you have a standard warm-up sequence that you use, use it for everything, including competition. This becomes a familiar part of the fencer's routine, and becomes a reassuring part of getting ready at competitions.

- Safety is a major concern. German studies show that as much as 40% of injuries that cause fencers to lose the remainder of the season come in warm-up. Ball games are especially problematic. Safe also includes appropriate for the age, physical condition, and psychological state of the fencers.

- Stretching should only follow activity that raises muscular readiness – never as a first activity, and never ballistic or static stretching. Ballistic stretching of muscles that are not fully ready has a high injury potential. Static stretching has been demonstrated to actually limit muscle performance under some conditions. Stretching is best done at the end of training or competition when the muscles are most ready and when it may help eliminate waste products from the muscles.

- Games must be sport specific – and must be controlled – a high percentage of injuries occur in warm-up games. Some games are dangerous on the face of it – a lunge to stomp on your opponent's foot game for example. Some games introduce movement patterns that are counterproductive in most situations – the catch the glove before it hits the floor game as an example (when was the last time you lunged at a falling object fully exposing your arm and upper torso in a competition?). And some games promote psychological dominance of your own fencers – the hand slap game is an example.

    - Look for ways to make common games more sport specific.

    - Ask yourself why you are doing the game – is this the best way to achieve this objective, given the available time you have for a lesson?

- If you use calisthenics make certain your knowledge of the techniques is current. We still see coaches using calisthenics that other sports long ago abandoned as dangerous – full deep knee bends are an example.

- Circuit or interval training is also good for warm-up activity. It can be made sports specific by incorporating fencing movements or fencing timing in the various activities. For example, a circuit can be constructed that has the fencer do footwork, point control exercises, response to opponent movement, etc. Interval training that mimics the flow of a bout with rest periods keyed to referee halt-to-fence periods is particularly useful.

Footwork

Footwork is simultaneously a sports specific warm-up, a way to build skills through repetition, and a tactical warm-up (through practice of specific footwork combinations). We can use a progression of footwork to go from coach initiated to fencer initiated activity, either in a single session or as a longer term progression from lesson to lesson. The difficulty and value increase as you move from least student autonomy to greatest student autonomy.

- Command footwork – the coach calls out the individual steps the student will execute, setting both the action and the speed. For example, "advance, retreat, advance, etc."

- Sets – the coach calls out specific combinations of footwork for the student to execute. Now the student has more control over the speed of execution. These combinations can be simply random, or they can be specific tactical combinations the fencer will execute. For example, "two advances, retreat, lunge," a common footwork trap.

- React to instructor – the coach varies the speed and distance, moving forward and backward, opens a line for the lunge, or lunges at the students, to trigger a mirror reaction. This is closer to bout conditions, but it does cost the students the initiative.

    - Make certain that your movements as the instructor are as realistic as possible and that will be what the fencer will see in competition. Otherwise you are training for stimuli that will not occur. For example, some instructors signal a lunge or other action by raising the left hand or the right hand. This trains students to watch for a cue the opponents will not do in a bout. A more realistic cue would be for the instructor to initiate an invitation easily seen by the students, for example, lowering the arm from high line to low line.

- Paired with other students – this exercise can start with one side or the other leading based on the instructor to call "left leads" or "right leads," allowing the student leading full initiative on speed, length, and timing of movement.

- No lead - the exercise can transition to "no lead" where students take the initiative and establish by their actions who is leading and who is reacting. This helps students develop their ability to control the flow of the bout and assists in learning ways to take over the action.

The level of footwork used in this period depends upon the capability of the fencers and the training objectives of the lesson.

The Main Body of the Lesson

The main body of the lesson is what we think of as a lesson – this is where we teach the student something new, train them in techniques they already know, make corrections, and generally think that we are doing our jobs as coaches. Actually the main body is part of a flow. If we have done our job, the warm-up activities and the footwork have been planned to lead the student to the main body.

The lesson should be progressive in nature so that each technique builds on the previous one and logically leads to another – even if only by explanation.

- Review the technique or tactics taught in a previous lesson that are applicable to the new technique. This does not have to be a long review, just enough so that the students will have the foundation for the new technique in mind. For example, if you are teaching a feint of straight thrust-disengage compound attack, do a quick review of straight thrust and a quick review of disengage, even if only by having the students do a number of each as a drill.

- Consider teaching the offense and the specific defense against that offense as a pair. For example, teach the straight thrust in 6th, and the parry of 6th and riposte together.

- Use a tactical wheel progression. Once you introduce the concept of tactics and the tactical wheel you can frame all of this in tactical as well as technical progression. Now the students can work pairs of action as a tactical wheel progression. For example, the drill starts with a simple attack with the other fencer executing a simple parry-riposte. At the next step, students have to execute a compound attack to defeat the parry.

Demonstrate the skills to be learned or how the skills are put together. If you are going to have students do a drill, demonstrate the drill before they do it, several times for beginners and intermediates.

Put the students to work – basic tool is the drill of which there are many types – at this level we will focus on:

- simple **LINE DRILLS**. As the name suggests the students are formed in a line from the coach's left to right, facing the coach.

    - For skills where the fencer will not require an opponent, have the students line up in a straight line, all facing forward. The line can move forward or backwards to execute fencing actions.

    - Where the fencer will need to work against other fencers have two lines facing each other at the appropriate distance. If there is an odd number of fencers, arrange the lines so that one fencer sits out a set, and rotate frequently. Alternatively, the instructor can fill the empty place and provide correction and fine tuning of the skill for each fencer who rotates through his or her position. Have a standard plan for how students move to their left or right to rotate positions. Using 5 executions as the point for rotation will expose the students to a number of opponents, and train the student to think in terms of 5 hits.

- **EXCHANGE DRILLS.** The exchange drill is a standard way to conduct drills. It has the advantage of requiring students to change roles multiple times, much as they will have to be prepared for both attack and defense in bouting.

  - One fencer is the attacker, one the defender. After each attack, the fencers change roles and execute the appropriate offense or defensive skill.

  - This format easily allows a full range of footwork by both fencers.

  - Exchange drills require supervision. Regardless of how well you prepared the drill with demonstration and instructions, in intermediate and beginner classes a sizeable percentage of the students will not be able to do even a simple drill the first time. Be prepared to lead them through the drill movement by movement, even guiding their blade actions with your hands.

Monitor what the students are doing and enforce discipline in the execution of the drill.

- Students will want to change any drill into something that meets their conception of what they should be doing. Ensure students do each set of movements as a discrete set, and do not degenerate into one long exchange. For example:

  Fencer A – attacks with a straight thrust
  Fencer B – parries in 6th and ripostes direct

  Fencer B – attacks with a straight thrust
  Fencer A – parries in 6th and ripostes direct

  Becomes:

  Fencer A – attacks with a straight thrust
  Fencer B – parries in 6th and ripostes direct
  Fencer A – parries in 6th and first counterripostes
  Fencer B – parries in 6th and second counterripostes
  And so on to the end of the drill period ...

- And understand that some students will want to take the action beyond the drill and into fighting a mini-bout. This outcome comes complete with actions that you have not included in the drill and with attempts to deliberately frustrate the other fencer's ability to complete the drill objectives. For example, a simple exchange intended to work the parry and riposte combination:

  Fencer A – attacks with a straight thrust

Fencer B – parries in 6th and ripostes direct

Becomes:

Fencer A – attacks with a straight thrust
Fencer B – parries in 6th and ripostes direct
Fencer A – parries in 6th and disengages into the low line to hit
The next time Fencer A – attacks with a disengage so that he can hit on the first action.
Fencer B – executes a circular parry and indirect riposte to hit so that she can hit.
And then ...

- None of these are good instructional outcomes. You must be prepared to stop, demonstrate, and enforce the drill as designed if the students are to learn.

These drills are **BLOCKED DRILLS**, a term you will need to remember. This means that one skill is repeated multiple times in the drill under the same conditions in a block of activity. Blocked drills are good for initial learning of a new skill. Research shows that they are also a key component of training skills for higher levels of performance.

Put the technique taught in its tactical context – you need to start teaching tactics as early as possible in your student's development. Fencing depends on their ability to use their physical attributes, use appropriate techniques well executed, and their brains to beat opponents.

- Show the tactical application, where and when it can be used, and where it sits on the tactical wheel.

    - Remember, a tactic is technique, plus footwork, plus distance, plus timing,

    - all in the context of the logic of the bout.

- Have students practice the complete skill in mini-bout setting (1 to 3 touch) or full bout setting. To ensure that the skill is used, set a ground rule that only the technique scores or that it is allowed a greater value. If you do a mini-bout, create a tactical scenario, such as (1) it is the first touch of the bout and whoever hits first wins the bout (statistically first touches bestow a significant advantage) or (2) the score is 3-4 and you are down, so fence to win using the technique (giving the other fencer the reversed problem that they are up 4-3).

Conclusion

Like the introduction, the lesson conclusion is an important transition. The fencers have met your objectives for this session; now you have to transition them physically and mentally to be prepared for the next lesson.

- Cool down the students with less intense drills transitioning in 5 or so repetitions to slow execution with limited footwork.

- If you intend to include stretching in your lesson, this is a good place for slow or static stretching.
- Do a quick review of 2-3 key points from the lesson that you want the students to remember.
- Ask for student questions and answer them. If no one asks any questions, ask the students one or two questions that emphasize the points you want them to take away.
- And do a next lesson motivation. This is as simple as telling them what the next lesson is and how it relates to this lesson.
- Finally, a formal salute and dismissal of the class.

Class Formations

Given a mass of students, you have to use some organizational structure that manages the space you have effectively. The common method of one straight line, or of several straight ranks, works, and works well, subject to several caveats.

- Put left handed students on the right side of the line as you look at them from the front. This allows the fencers to watch you without having to twist their heads to look over their shoulders. Position yourself as close to the transition point in the line from left to right handed as is practical. Reverse these instructions if you are left handed. In addition to considering left or right handedness you may need to arrange students by height so that smaller fencers' vision is not blocked by taller ones.
- A long line creates difficulty in hearing instructions and in seeing the instructor, especially for those at the ends. It also may force the instructor to demonstrate techniques more than once, and to move more to supervise student practice. Much like airline cabin staff demonstrating safety procedures, you may be stationed toward one end of the line to mimic the demonstration another coach gives toward the other end.
- Multiple ranks can work well for skills that do not require a partner, but students need to be able to move their position left or right to see the instructor through the line in front. In practical terms, when you have three lines, the rear rank will have a lot of difficulty seeing what is going on at the front.
- Some types of drills and instructions will require the fencers to all move in the same direction. For these, make certain there is sufficient clearance between the ranks for safety, and that there is sufficient clearance behind the rear rank to avoid backing into the wall at full speed.
- Some types of drills and instructions will require fencers to work facing other fencers, generally in pairs. For these, make certain that the pairings are of people of skill levels that make sense for the exercise (unless you plan to rotate the line after a set number of executions). This may mean that you have to do a bit of shifting at the start. Consider also the issue of whether you want left-handers facing left-handers or right-handers.

- In paired drills if you intend to rotate students to face new partners it is important to establish a standard rotation direction that is followed every time you have students change partners. Rotation has the fencers shift one place to the right or left when it is time to change partners; the fencers on the end of the line in the direction of shift cross to the other side. It becomes second nature for the students, eliminating a lot of confusion and wasted time.

- In every case allow enough room for the instructor to safely circulate among the fencers and make corrections.

- A circle or an arc may be excellent positioning in small groups where you want to be able to quickly move from student to student.

Instructor Positioning

Instructor positioning is an important part of any group teaching situation. You need to be where the students can see and hear you clearly. This means:

- generally position yourself with your right handed fencers to your left and the left handed fencers to your right (or the reverse if you are left handed). If the left handed are on your right, this means line up facing the first right handed fencer. This lets students follow you without having to look over their shoulders.

- position yourself so that you can see every fencer. Don't count on them positioning themselves so that they can see you.

- be relatively static in front of the formation when you demonstrate a skill, either alone or with a partner, move in the same direction as the formation when you are doing footwork drills, and circulate through the formation when the students are learning skills or practicing two person drills.

- watch your own safety - while you are correcting a problem with one student, be sure that you are out of lunge range of the fencer behind him or her. There are few things more unpredictable than a student with a sword, and many students seem to think that basic safety rules do not apply when the instructor is in front of them.

Lesson Planning

Lesson planning is a key part of teaching anything, including fencing. When you assist a coach in a class you need to understand what the plan is for that class – what will be taught, in what order, what role you will play, and how long a time you have allotted for your activity. Some coaches have detailed written plans for every lesson they teach in group classes – many rely on years of practice and run classes out of their mental plan.

You, however, are new to this and need to have thought about what you are to do, what order it will be in, and how you will complete your task. If there is a written plan that specifies what drill at what time, identify with the coach what is your part and ask any questions you need to ask to clarify your responsibilities. But if there is not, you need to be ready to make your own mini-plan for your parts, perhaps on something as small as a note pad or 3x5 index card.

Lesson plans help you document what you have taught, use that documentation to plan future lessons, make sure that you do not forget key items, and keep you from turning left at the fence and going across the fields in the wrong direction.

- All lessons should be planned. Even quick interventions should have a standard plan that you have used so often that it is automatic.

- Identify objectives. What are you trying to teach and what do you want the student to be able to do?

- Plan activities. What steps will you use to teach the skill? What key things must you not forget?

- Make plans progressive so that they build from known to unknown, simple to complex.

- Plans can be 5 minutes thought and a 3 by 5 card, or they can be a detailed computer generated plan in a standard series of plans instructors your club use.

- Keep your lesson plans – you will be assigned to teach the same activities again. In addition this serves as documentation of what you taught. Date the plan and record the participants in your handwriting on the plan sheet. This will be crucial to document what you taught in the case of litigation.

Key items to consider including in your lesson plan include:

- what activity comes before yours,
- how long you have to do your assignment,
- what you are to do – what skill you will teach, what drill you will lead,
- key points for any introductory remarks,
- any added details – for example, footwork starting with advance and retreat, add lunge on dropped arm, accelerate for faster actions for about 2 minutes, decelerate to work students on retreat lunge, relaxed advances and retreats, end,
- key points for summation, and
- what activity follows yours.

Print in large print, condense thoughts to one or two words to key your memory, and keep the card where you can easily refer to it. With practice, this process should take you no more than 2-3 minutes. You will find that the process not only helps organize what you are doing, but it sets it in your mind so that you rarely have to refer to your plan.

Issues to Address

Always consider the following issues in planning and teaching:

- move from known to unknown, simple to complex, slow to fast.

- emphasize relaxation as the key to speed and correct application. Culturally we believe we are not working unless we are expending a lot of effort and force. This results in raised pulse rates, the loss of fine motor control, and slow erratic execution.

- safety cannot be overemphasized:

    - yours – you are in a room full of the most dangerous animal on earth – the fencing student armed with steel – watch your back and your eyes.

    - theirs – keep attuned to correct equipment, movement patterns, where people are pointing their blades.

    - emphasize some element of safety during each class.

- there are a lot of younger students with significant developmental issues – make sure you understand how to work with ADHD, Asperger's syndrome, etc. students.

- heavy hitters. Put an early stop to this; it is both unpleasant and unproductive in terms of technique. Much heavy hitting can be corrected by working with students to use correct timing in their execution or to relax (rather than tighten) in their movement

- deal with discipline problems and authority challengers out of earshot of the rest of the fencers. If they cannot modify their behavior it is reasonable to ask them to leave to ensure that other students will have a good learning environment

- minimize talking – emphasize doing. Information is delivered to students orally by talking and visually by demonstration. However, students require thousands of repetitions to be able to perform a skill to a reasonable standard under pressure. The martial arts generally use a figure of 10,000 to 50,000 repetitions for skill mastery.

Corrections

Correcting student performance is an important part of teaching and training the athlete. Good corrective practices lead to the athlete discovering the best way to execute a technique for his or her body. Poorly done correction may actually increase the degree and frequency of incorrect performance of the skill, along with raising student frustration levels.

Corrections can be general or specific.

- General corrections are those that you make to the entire group when you observe a common problem in execution of a skill - you stop the exercise and demonstrate again the correct technique.

- Specific corrections are made individual by individual. You stop at one student, quickly correct that error with your weapon and/or non-weapon hand, set the skill with two or three performances, and move on.

When doing corrections there are four key ground rules:

- first – at the start of learning a new technique or a new drill, use general corrections, even for individual problems. If one student has a problem understanding and performing, others in the group have the same problem.

- second - demonstrate correct performance. Remember that people learn movement largely through visual cues. Poor modeling may result in poor performance by the students. And showing the students the wrong way to perform the skill may well fix the wrong way, rather than the right way, in their minds.

- third - praise good performance. Positive reinforcement goes a long way in motivating the student.

- fourth - frame corrections in positive ways that will make sense to and encourage the student. A soft "here is how to do this better" is generally more successful than a stern "you are screwing up again."

Do not become frustrated if students are unable to at first perform correctly. Learning is a long-term process and improvements show up gradually. The following guidelines will help improve your success in helping your fencers learn.

- Don't correct too early. Many performance errors are discovered by students and self-corrected. Allow 3 or 4 incorrect repetitions before stepping in with a correction. If the student self-corrects there is a lower incidence of incorrect performances in the future.

- Don't hypercorrect – students can process one correction at a time. Traditionally fencing coaches have been expected to jump on every technical error and fix it as soon as it happens, the "drop your point, extend your arm more, turn the foot into line, use the back leg, make sure you drop your back arm, keep your head level, watch the opponent's reaction ..." correction. No student can correct all of these errors at one time. If you correct one error each session, and the student comes once a week, you will correct 52 problems a year – a lot of problems.

- Focus on how to make performance better – not on how the student is failing to do it perfectly. Perfection comes with 10,000-50,000 repetitions. You will not get there in one lesson.

- Make the correction and move on quickly. If you are the only person supervising the activity, you can get caught up in a correction, work on it for 5 or 6 minutes, and the rest of the class has finished their work and wandered off out of control.

- Use group corrections where possible. This is particularly appropriate if several students are having the same problem. Group corrections will correct enough of the students to allow you to focus on the hard core cases.

- Build a culture where students help each other correct. This is very important. Students will go along with almost anything on the part of their practice partner, either because they do not know themselves or because they do not want to appear confrontational. The result is that you have several pairs of students doing something that may or may not be fencing, but that certainly is not what you want them to be doing. And in the process they learn nothing. Make students responsible for helping their partners learn. This helps learning and it builds cohesion as fencers learn to count on their team mates.

- Fix distance and extension problems early. These can become the basis of other faults later.

Always try to find the root cause for the problem you observe. This may take several corrections before you understand exactly what the student is doing and why they are doing it. If you have to correct an action multiple times over several lessons, something more than what you think is happening is causing the problem. It may be attitude, it may be structural, or it may be the lead in actions to the technique. You will only find these if you look for them.

17. Individual Lessons

The teaching duties for Assistant Moniteurs also include short individual lessons, mini-lessons in effect, that guide improved student performance. Such lessons may be as short as 1 minute, and are normally incorporated in the group lesson to correct problems during drills or bouting. However, this section will familiarize you with the general format of individual lessons, as you may be asked to work with a student who needs more than a short intervention.

The Teaching Position

The teaching position for lessons is different from the fencing position. This reduces wear and tear on your body and allows you to move quickly enough to challenge students who are faster than you are.

- Stand relaxed and upright.

- Control your blade position so that it is at a realistic height for the movement you are performing. Inexperienced coaches will execute actions with the arm and blade at their shoulder height; you need to adjust arm height in your attacks to simulate the arm height in a lunge. And adjust overall arm height downward as needed for young fencers.

- Keep the back arm out of the way, hanging down straight. Any other position becomes a potential distraction to the student.

- Your footwork is closer to walking than to the traditional advance or retreat; lunges are delivered as a strong step forward.

The Individual Lesson

The full individual lesson is structured in much the same format as the group lesson. This serves as the model for any individual instruction, including the short assessment or check lesson an Assistant Moniteur may be asked to give.

This lesson has three parts: Introduction – Main Body – Conclusion. Now the instructor is the single training partner, and is the one creating the cues for the student to hit. Most lessons an Assistant Moniteur is expected to be able to teach are simple, single action lessons.

- The Introduction includes a quick statement of what the lesson will cover, warming the student up with blade and footwork to increase both physical and psychological readiness, and a quick review of material already known that leads into the lesson subject.

- The main body concentrates on demonstrating the skill to be learned, slow blocked repetition until the skill is clearly understood, and then building speed while maintaining form.

    - This is the model the United States Fencing Coaches Association teaches, and this is probably most effective at the Assistant Moniteur level. Moniteurs in their own teaching, as opposed to in examinations, should be prepared to introduce choices once the student has demonstrated the ability to perform the skill, as research shows this is the most effective way to improve learning.

- The Conclusion ends with a cool down exercise to relax the student, typically a well-known skill or the skill learned executed with decreasing speed and less involved footwork. End with a short oral review of what has been covered and any questions the student may have.

Initially the individual lesson is all instructor led, with the instructor setting all of the parameters: action, distance, timing, initiation by cue.

As you develop coaching skills learn to transition to at least partly student led. The greater the degree of student leadership, the more realistic the lesson is and the better the training received. Students can be given the lead by allowing them to determine when to attack, what footwork to use to manage the distance, and even what technique to use in the attack.

Many coaches have adopted the practice of having the student hold the point on the target until the instructor drives the blade up with his or her weapon. Supposedly this teaches the student to fix the point. In reality it is a completely unrealistic movement combination that teaches the student to delay recovery based on a cue that it is unlikely an opponent will provide. Do not whack the blade as a cue to recover. The hit, or miss, is the cue to recover.

Cues

The coach provides cues for action – the individual lesson is driven by cues. Although you may have to orally explain or correct, the more time you spend talking, the fewer the repetitions the fencer will perform. So the general principle is less talk – more doing. Use your cues to talk for you.

At the Assistant Moniteur level these may be blade or footwork cues. These may be blade cues to open or close a line or to search for the blade, footwork cues to cause distance control or trigger an attack, or body movement cues to create openings or trigger reactions. Cues should be relatively wide and obvious for beginners and become smaller and more realistic for competitive fencers. Try to select cues that are not ambiguous and that relate directly to the actions you teach.

Assessment or Check Lessons

The most common lesson the Assistant Moniteur will teach is the Assessment or Check Lesson. This is a short lesson delivered to assess student learning or to provide technical corrections as part of an overall group lesson.

- The focus is one error, one technique, one tactic – one of one thing – per lesson. Do not hypercorrect.

- Lesson duration is no more than 1 to 3 minutes. Short is better, and allows you to make more interventions per session. In addition, when you are focused on one student or one pair, other students can deviate significantly from the planned activity.

- Diagnose performance. Identify the core problem. Very often this is not what you see, but may be a posture issue, a footwork alignment problem, or a problem in initial execution. Watch what the student is doing carefully and work backward to the fundamental movement.

- Correct errors. Demonstrate correct execution, and generally do not show the student what they are doing wrong (as often as not they will remember the bad performance rather than the correct one). Uses guided movement as needed.

- Repetitions. Have the student execute a number of repetitions. Make any fine tuning corrections as needed, staying with the original problem you chose to correct.

- The goal is for the student to make 3 to 5 correct performances of the skill.

- Repeat the one key concept you want the student to remember. This statement should relate directly to the reason you intervened to teach the lesson in the first place – for example, "remember, smooth full extension of the arm."

- And then move on. Return the student to the activity in which he or she was engaged. And then observe for more situations requiring intervention, or work with the next waiting student, or move on to the next activity.

Other Types of Individual Lessons

As you develop as a coach, have your professional coach teach you the particular types of lessons used by more advanced coaches. At the Moniteur level you will need to be able to teach technical lessons. If you go to competitions with your fencers, you need to understand the warmup lesson. The five minute lesson is a great tool to use to give short, complete lessons as part of a larger class or practice. And as you work toward Prevot you will need to be able to do any of these formats:

- **FIVE MINUTE LESSON**. This is a German evolution of the Tauberbischofheim lesson. It is an intense, short, focused lesson that works one technique for maximum repetitions with a variety of footwork. The short time period allows the student to maintain focus throughout the lesson. When used in a practice or class session with every coach teaching the same lesson, it maximizes the number of fencers who can receive individual attention each day.

- **TRAINING LESSON**. This lesson is designed to: (1) build proficiency in known techniques, (2) develop tactical applications of skills, (3) increase the ability to fence eyes open, (4) train in reacting to logical choices presented by the opponent in reaction to your action, and (5) to develop stamina and fighting spirit. The focus is on improving the execution of skills the fencer already knows and uses.

- **TECHNICAL or TEACHING LESSON**. This is an instruction lesson to introduce and develop technical skills in one or more techniques that are logically related to each other. The lesson is at a relatively low stress level with a focus on developing correct movement patterns.

- **BOUTING LESSON**. The bouting lesson is a tactical lesson designed to test technique and its tactical application in bout-like conditions. The coach acts as an opponent would, and the fencer is expected to apply a selected range of techniques in the correct distance, timing, and tactical progression in the bout.

- **WARM-UP LESSON**. This lesson is delivered at the competition site, ideally ending 20-30 minutes before the fencer is expected to fence. Its intent is to prepare the fencer physically and mentally for competition. The focus is on bringing the fencer up to full readiness with techniques that are well known and that he or she expects to use in bouts on that day. Unless specifically indicated for a particular opponent, no new or rarely practiced techniques should be included.

18. Basic Rules of Fencing

The rules of fencing are published by the Federation Internationale d'Escrime (the International Fencing Federation, or FIE), and the complete text in English (with additions to indicate differences in the international and United States rules) is available online at the USA Fencing website. As a coach you must have read and thoroughly learned the current rules, and you must keep up with rule changes. As important is how the rules are being interpreted by local, national level, and international referees (and often there is wide variance on even simple concepts, such as when the attack starts). If you do not know the rules, you cannot teach your students how to protect their interests on the strip.

One of the responsibilities of the Assistant Moniteur can be to referee practice bouts in the club. In this context you can work with an abbreviated set of rules. Note that I have included references to the specific paragraphs for these rules; some fencers and some referees do not know the rules and invent rules based on their conception of what they should be. It is helpful to know what the real rules state, and where to find those statements.

- The fencing strip is 14 meters long by 1.5 to 2 meters wide. On guard lines are 2 meters from the center, and fencers come on guard behind these lines at the start of the bout and after each touch is scored. Warning lines are 2 meters from the end of the strip. A safety overrun of 1.5 to 2 meters should be available behind each end of the strip *(rules t.13 and t.14 and figures 1 and 2).*

- Not every club has sufficient floor space for full sized strips. However, any shortened strip using for training should preserve the relationship of the on guard lines to the center of the strip and of the warning lines to the end of the strip. There are no requirements for separation from adjacent strips, and many clubs try to put as many strips as possible in their space, in a few cases with only a foot of clearance between them, risking collisions or weapon hits across strip boundaries. An absolute minimum safe separation of practice strips is 3 feet.

- Bouts are fenced for 5 touches in 3 minutes of fencing time *(rule t.30).* If the score is tied at the end of 3 minutes, the referee flips a coin, and fencing continues for one added minute. If at the end of that period neither fencer has scored, the winner of the coin toss wins the bout *(rule o.17 para 2b).* Refer to the rules for time limits and touches for direct elimination, team, and Pentathlon Epee (the Pentathlon rule book in this case).

- The referee should ensure that the fencers are wearing proper protective equipment and that their jackets and masks are correctly fastened *(rules t.35 para. 2 and t.43).*

- Bouts are started by having the fencers salute *(rule t.87 para. 3)* and come on guard at the on guard lines and in the center of the strip *(rule t.17).* The command "fence" starts the action, and "halt" stops it *(rule t.18 paras. 1 and 2).* Actions that start after the halt cannot result in award of a touch *(rule t.18 para. 3).* Fencers return to the on guard line position after each award of a touch. If no hit is awarded because a touch did not occur or hit off target, the fencers take distance from each other in the center of the strip and fence from where the action halted *(rule t.17).*

- At foil and saber the fencers may not come into physical contact. The fencer causing such contact (corps a corps) is warned (Yellow card) and then has a touch scored against him or her (Red card). At epee corps a corps is permitted without penalty, but the action is stopped when the fencers are in body contact. Forcing a corps a corps to avoid being hit or jostling is warned and then receives a touch penalty in all weapons *(rule t.20).*

- If a fencer steps off the side of the strip with both feet, the other fencer will advance one meter, and the offending fencer will take distance from this new position. If a fencer steps over the rear line with both feet a touch is awarded against the fencer *(rule t.27)*. However, if a fencer steps over the side boundary with one foot, the fencer who stepped off retreats one meter, and the fencers take distance *(rule t.28.1)*.

- The target in each of the weapons is different. In simple terms:

    - in foil, the target is the torso, not including the head, arms or legs, but including the back above the line of the upper point of the hips. The bib of the mask below a horizontal line drawn 1.5 to 2 centimeters below the chin of the mask is also part of the target *(rule t.47)*.

    - in sabre, the target is the torso above the line of the upper point of the hip bones, including the arms and head, but not including the hands *(rule t.71)*.

    - in epee the entire body is target *(rule t.62)*.

- The referee determines the right of way in foil and saber and the priority of the hit in epee (if electric scoring apparatus is not being used) *(rule t.42)*.

    - Right of way belongs to the fencer initiating an attack by extending the weapon arm with the weapon continuously threatening the target, and is retained until the attack either misses or is parried *(rules t.56 through t.60 and t.76 through t.80)*. If both fencers arrive on target, the fencer with right of way wins the touch. Referees tend to allow a fair amount of latitude in interpreting what "continuously threatening the target" means, but the attack must start with a forward movement of the weapon arm toward valid target, even if that movement is small and visible only to the referee.

    - If the attack with the right of way is parried, the defender will gain the right of way by immediately riposting (an attack itself), which retains the right of way until parried or until it misses *(rules t.57 and t.79)*.

        - A parry is a symbolic act and does not require that the opponent's blade be removed from the line and held away so that it cannot hit. It is impossible for a referee to determine from the side lines that a blade was deflected a certain amount. Even a light fast parry will deflect the blade sufficiently. In all weapons an opponent's attack that is blocked by the forte or bell of the defender's weapon should be considered parried.

        - If an attack is parried, and the riposte is not immediate, the first offensive action after the parry seizes the right of way.

        - When the attack ends in right of way weapons is open to interpretation, but in general is interpreted as when it obviously reaches the end of its movement or when the opponent is no longer reacting to it.

    - At epee the first hit to arrive scores the touch. If the referee cannot determine a time differences between the two hits in dry fencing (or audibly when using training buzz boxes), both fencers are hit. Obviously in fully electric epee with a scoring machine, two lights indicates a simultaneous hit against both fencers.

- Fencers cannot score hits if they hit while stepping off the strip with both feet *(rules t.26 para 2 and t.27)*, after they pass their opponents *(rule t.21 para 4)*, or if the action lands after the expiration of time *(rule t.32)*. However, actions can score if they are part of an attack that lands with one foot off the lateral boundary of the strip *(rule t.26 para 3)*, or if initiated before the referee calls halt when time has not expired *(rule t.18)*. It is important to understand that when the referee calls halt is in the mind of the referee, and results from a condition that requires stopping the bout. There is a time lag from recognition of the situation to the call for a halt, essentially referee reaction time.

- A fencer who runs off the strip in front of the opponent or passes an opponent may be hit by an immediate continuous riposte or counterattack executed as part of the action in which the opponent passed *(rule t.21 para 4)* or left the strip *(rule t.26 para 2)*.

- Fencers must fence in a controlled, orderly, and safe way. Falling in an attempt to score a hit, turning the back on the opponent, removing the mask before the referee calls halt, and disorderly fencing should all penalized by a warning (Yellow card) and then by the scoring of a hit against the fencer (Red card) *(rule t.120)*.

  - Although not provided for in the FIE rules, training bouts in the club should also require for safety that fencers remain in a position to defend themselves until the referee has called a halt and the other fencer has stopped fencing. Also fencers should not turn to look at the scoring apparatus when they believe a hit has arrived.

- Fencers must be courteous to the referee and to each other. Jostling or running into opponents is warned (Yellow card) and then results in a touch scored against the initiator (Red card). Deliberate brutal heavy hitting, bad sportsmanship, throwing items, berating the referee, or other versions of the temper tantrum, should receive an immediate penalty of loss of the bout (Black card) *(rule t.120)*. It may justify telling the fencer to sit out the rest of practice. This may well be harsher than the penalty imposed by a referee in a competition, but if you are to train fencers to act appropriately in competition, the tendency to act in outrageous ways should be dealt with very firmly, early on in the fencer's development. In a club situation warnings are relatively ineffective if not backed with real sanctions.

- At the end of a bout the fencers return to their on guard lines, salute, and then advance to shake hands *(rule t.87 para 3)*. The rules requiring the salute and handshake are enforced and the failure to do so can result in disqualification. They should be built into practice bouts from the very start of training to ensure that they are an automatic part of the fencer's routine on the strip.

19. Refereeing Club Bouts

Every coach should be able to serve as a referee for either dry or electric bouts fenced in the club. Not only does this help the club run internal competitions and help your fellow fencers train under realistic conditions, but it also helps you develop your understanding of the role and influence of the referee in bouts. Even though bouts in the club are primarily training bouts, the referee should perform his or her duties in the same manner as a referee in regular competitions. The basic responsibilities of a referee in club bouts include:

- before the bout the referee checks the fencers' weapons, uniform, and equipment, and performs the standard tests that verify the weapons are functioning correctly and that the uniform is worn safely. In foil the test is a weight test (500 grams – the spring in the point must return the weight after it is depressed); in epee the test includes testing for finger tightness of the barrel of the point, visual check that screws are present, the weight (750 grams), and the shims for clearance (1 mm) and for minimum travel (0.5 mm). Fencers must wear a plastron (also known as an underarm protector); female fencers must wear a chest protector. Doing these checks helps establish the routine of competition in the fencers' minds, makes the bout closer to the competitive environment, and catches equipment that needs maintenance.

- calling the fencers to "on guard," asking if they are "ready," and giving the command to "fence." Fencers are not required to reply to the "ready" question – if no one says they are not ready, the assumption is that both fencers are ready. When a hit arrives or is believed to have arrived, a fencer steps off the strip, or a dangerous situation develops, the referee calls "halt."

- looking for the flow of the action. From which side does the attack initiate? Is there a stop hit that arrives in time? Is the attack parried or does it fall short? When does the flow reverse in the other direction?

- describing the action as needed to determine right of way in foil and sabre or priority in epee and the arrival of hits. Referee description of the action may be solely by the use of hand signals. These include:

    - the arm partly extended parallel to the strip and the hand turned fingers pointing down – on the side of the initial attack.
    - the arm extended toward the other fencer – an offensive action against that fencer (attack, stop hit, remise, riposte).
    - the arm pumped horizontally – indicates preparation of the attack by the fencer on the side the pump is directed toward.
    - the arm extended with the forearm vertically upward – a touch by the fencer on the side of the raised arm.
    - the vertical forearm wagged upward from side to side – the attack directed toward that side does not arrive.
    - the forearm wagged from side to side downwards – the attack directed toward that side arrives not valid.
    - both forearms wagged hand down – no touch awarded, usually for simultaneous action.
    - the forearms crossed vertically and horizontally – the fencer on that side parries the action.

- the arm extended with the index finger extended – a point in line.

- using the electric scoring apparatus to determine whether a hit arrived on target, or in foil also off target. If judges are used in a dry bout, the referee polls the judges to determine whether a hit arrived. Each judge has one vote, and the referee one and one-half votes. Judges and the referee vote "yes," "yes but not valid" in foil, "no," and "abstain" (which does not count as a vote in determining whether or not there was a hit). Judges on each side are responsible for watching the opposite fencer.

- positioning himself or herself so the scoring apparatus is visible (when fencing electric) and moving with the action so he or she can clearly see the progression of the fencing phrase. This requires the referee to be at least 6 and preferably 9 or more feet from the edge of the piste. If one fencer is left handed that fencer should be on the referee's left.

  - Note that correct positioning for the referee is difficult in those clubs that pack as many strips as possible into limited space. A referee standing close to the action cannot see the overall flow, a task made much more difficult when the scoring machine is hung over the strip.

- when no hit is awarded, positioning the fencers at equal distance from the center point of the action and in the middle of the piste.

- directing the fencers to change ends when one fencer has scored three touches in dry bouts (unless only one is left handed). This equalizes the lighting and the judging. Because of the electrical apparatus this is not done in electrical fencing.

- maintaining order in the bout and making certain fencing proceeds quickly.

- identifying infractions of the rules and awarding penalties.

- testing weapons and equipment and identifying the cause of failures when there is any malfunction.

However, the most important function of the referee is to be impartial, to award touches as he or she sees them, and to manage the bout honestly without favoritism or malice. This is particularly important in training bouts; without an impartial calling of the action, the fencer has no idea how he or she is progressing technically and tactically.

20. Fencer Classification

Fencer classification is a complicated subject, and one which you may be asked about by fencers who are interested in competition. Understanding the following section requires reference to the current year's edition of USA Fencing's Athlete Handbook, available at the website http://usfencing.org, currently in the Document's section of the Resources pull down on the front page.

Competitive fencers are classified by USA Fencing into six lettered ranks. All fencers start as Unclassified, denoted by a U. As fencers become more experienced and develop their abilities they may be promoted to E, D, C, B, and finally A classifications based on the place they achieve in USA Fencing amateur competitions, the size of those events, the number of classified fencers participating, and the number and classification of fencers in the final rounds. Fencer classifications are specific to the weapon and must be renewed within 4 years to remain at the same level. If the fencer does not achieve the same rating to renew the classification, the classification decays one letter and is reset at the new year. For example, a C earned in 2001 (C2001), will decay to a D in 2005 (D2005).

To understand the classification chart which contains each of the requirements (located as an appendix in the Athlete Handbook), work from left to right.

- Find the number of fencers less than or equal to the number entered in the competition.
- Then from those choices find the number and rank of classified fencers equal to or less than the number entered in the completion.
- Then from those choices find the number and rank of classified fencers in the final 8 or 12 fencers.
- And the last column tells you how many of what level of classification are awarded.

For example, 31 fencers are entered in a tournament: 1 A, 1 B, 3 Cs, 2 Ds, 2 Es, and 22 Us. In the final 8 there are 1 A, 1 B, 2 Cs, 1 D, and 3 Us.

- The meet total of 31 fencers yields the possibility of a C2, B2, or A2 rating
- The combination of 1A and 1B is equal to 2 Bs and, with 3 Cs and 2 Ds, is equal to a B2 rating.
- And we were lucky that the final 8 included 1 A and 1 B, equal to 2 Bs, and 2 Cs.
- As a result first place could renew a B (but it does nothing for his A), second through fourth can renew or earn a C, fifth through eighth a D, and ninth through twelfth an E.

Competitions are similarly rated in two different ways. Our discussion above introduced you to the classification chart which determines both the possible outcomes for fencers and the actual rating of the competitions themselves. The full range of ratings for competitions is:

- NR – not rated with no classification awarded
- E1 – maximum classification awarded E
- D1 – maximum classification awarded D
- C1, C2, C3 – maximum classification awarded C
- B1, B2, B3, B4 – maximum classification awarded B
- A1, A2, A3, A4 – maximum classification awarded A.

The highest classification that can be earned at the competition is reflected in the competition's rating. Thus, at a C2 event, the highest classification that can be earned or renewed is a C.

When a fencer registers for a competition listed on the Fencing Results and Events Database (FRED), FRED provides a predicted rating based on the entries. The actual rating of a competition is not determined until the final 8 or final 12 fencers are determined, and that rating depends on having the minimum number of fencers, the correct minimum mix of classified fencers, and the right minimum mix of classifications in the final 8 or 12 fencers.

There are also four divisions of Senior tournaments (open to fencers age 13 and above) based on the classifications of fencers who are eligible to enter the event:

- Division I – open to fencers classified as A, B, or C and other qualifying requirements in the Athlete's Handbook
- Division IA – open to fencers meeting qualifying requirements in the Athlete's Handbook
- Division II – open to fencers classified as C, D, E, and U
- Division III – open to fencers classified as D, E, and U

Open events are open to all fencers who meet the minimum age requirement of 13, unless otherwise limited

At the individual USA Fencing division level it is common for events to be listed as open to fencers of a certain classification or lower classifications, for example, a C and Under tournament.

Finally fencers are classified by age groups. In the Veterans, Youth, and Cadet and Junior age groups a range of competitions are held that restrict entry to members of the age group. Age Groups generally are based upon the fencer's birth year at the start of the season, and the specific year ranges are published each year by USA Fencing for national tournaments and a separate table for the Summer Nationals and its qualifying events. The age groups are:

- Veterans 70 – age 70 and above
- Veterans 60 – age 60-69
- Veterans 50 – age 50-59
- Veterans – age 40 and above
- Senior – Divisions 1, 1a, II, III, and wheelchair, age 13 and above
- Junior (U20/U19) – under age 20 (or age 19 for Summer Nationals)
- Cadet (U17/U16) – under age 17 (or age 16 for Summer Nationals)
- Y14 – age 14-11
- Y12 – age 12-9
- Y10 – age 10-7

21. Basic Fencing Statistics

In other sports, athletes, coaches, and fans can rattle off in great detail all of the elements of performance that are considered important for even little known teams and players. The level of sophistication of the analysis and the tactical impact of the data is significant. This suggests that as a coach there are things you need to know about your fencer's performance.

Fencing is a game of numbers. More victories, more touches for, fewer touches against rule competitions. One touch, leading to one victory, as opposed to no victories, can make the difference as to whether you make the cut for the direct elimination round in major tournaments. One indicator can move you five or six places up the seed in a large competition. And yet very few coaches do any statistical analysis of fencer performance as the basis for coaching. Given that numbers are important, it seems obvious that tracking numbers should be important to fencer development.

At the Assistant Moniteur level you should probably be most interested in the numbers you can influence, fencer performance in practice. Getting the data needed depends on two things, both of which are somewhat against the grain of what fencers want to do.

First, you must insist that fencers fence actual bouts (5 touches for pool and for Youth 10 and 12 direct elimination, 10 for Veterans, 15 for direct elimination, 1 for Pentathlon Epee) as part of their practice activity. "Let's just fence some hits" is probably better than having the fencers run laps (a future handbook will point out the bad effects of this), but not by much. The task in competition is to win the bout. Winning a bout is a combination of the strategy of the competition, the tactical choices made to deal with an opponent, and the techniques employed. The more of these elements present, the better the training, which is why the Tauberbischofheim model (when its fencers dominated world competition) was to fence a complete pool every practice, with the results feeding back into future training activity. You do not train to fight bouts in competition unless you fight bouts in practice.

Second, you must insist that fencers record the results of their bouts on a daily bout form. This is the only way you will get the data that appears on the score sheet in competition.

The data you gather in this way can be examined with some fairly sophisticated techniques. However, on a day to day and weekly to monthly basis, simple measurements can provide you with useful data for each fencer:

- the number of bouts fenced,
- the number of bouts won,
- total touches scored,
- total touches received, and
- indicators (touches scored minus touches received).

The number of bouts fenced is an indicator of:

- willingness to work (versus the perception of fencing as a social activity),
- the ability to fence a bout in the time allowed in competition (fencers who take 10 minutes for a 5 touch bout in sabre are not ready for prime time),

- conditioning, and
- fighting spirit.

Trends in numbers of bouts won for an individual indicate overall changing performance against the population of fencers to which they are exposed.

Trends in touches scored indicate the effectiveness of the fencer's offensive and counteroffensive actions.

Trends in touches received indicate the effectiveness of the fencer's defensive and counteroffensive actions.

Trends in indicators indicate the overall balance of the combined hitting and defensive effectiveness against opponents. The indicator can be divided by the number of bouts fenced to show the average by which the fencer wins or loses bouts, a useful guide to how much of a change is needed to make the next step in overall performance.

There is a second part to this. If you as a coach pay attention to these numbers and review them regularly with your athletes, eventually they will also start to pay attention. This is vital to their development as better fencers.

22. Maintenance

Each fencer is responsible for ensuring that his or her equipment is in safe and serviceable condition. That is inferred in the general statement in the rules of the sport that fencers fence at their own risk. However, this is does not remove your duty to your students who are paying for a service - as an instructor you bear two responsibilities. First, you must ensure that fencers in the salle or club are wearing proper equipment. This is part of your basic responsibility to maintain a safe environment. Second, you must ensure that the club's equipment is serviceable, well maintained, and safe. This is part of the club's responsibility to provide safe equipment. If the club provides equipment, it cannot expect to provide unsafe equipment and escape liability, especially with beginners who are not aware of, and trained in, the rules governing equipment.

General Checks for all Fencers

Before fencing you should always check fencers' equipment and clothing. Some of this can be done quickly by visual inspection of students as they come onto the fencing floor. Some can be done by asking questions or in general conversation. As a general rule you do not want to put your hands on the fencer to check clothing items without specifically asking for permission, and you really do not want to do this for fencers under age 18 without a parent or an independent witness present, and without the parent understanding the process. Never put your hand inside a fencer's clothing to check items – have them open jackets to show you plastrons, and to knock on their own breast protectors. Look for:

- mask - the bib is secure with no holes, the restraining strap fastens securely across the back, the tongue is tight enough to prevent the mask coming off the fencer's head, the mesh is in good condition with no corrosion or dents.

- jacket - the jacket fits and covers 10 centimeters below the waist of the knickers when the fencer is on guard; the jacket zips in the back or closes away from the opponent's sword; the jacket is in good condition with no tears or holes and with all stitching secure; and the jacket is clean.

- plastron - the plastron (or underarm protector) is in good condition with no tears or holes, its securing straps are secure, and the plastron is the appropriate size for the fencer.

- glove - the glove is in good condition with no tears or holes, the glove covers over the jacket sleeve approximately half way up the fencer's forearm.

- breast plates - breast plates are appropriately sized for the fencer and correctly positioned. This is a real problem with the standard cups designed to be inserted in jacket pockets – the cups provide limited protection, and the fencer is at the mercy of where the manufacturer put the pockets to hold them. Encourage female fencers to transition to appropriately sized torso plates as soon as possible.

- knickers – knickers, or pants, are in good repair with no holes or tears; knickers are clean; if the knickers open to the front, the opening is covered by the cuissard of the jacket; and if the knickers open to the side, the opening is away from the opponent's weapon. If the beginner is wearing other types of pants, they should meet the same general requirements as for knickers and should be of strong enough fabric to protect the legs. Sweat pants generally do not meet this requirement.

- socks – stockings cover the entire leg below the knickers; stockings are in good condition with no rips or holes; and stockings are clean.

- shoes - shoes are either fencing shoes or similar flat soled athletic shoes, tied, with adequate protection for the weapon leg heel, and with the sole in good condition. The flatter the sole the better; shoes with significantly raised heels change the foot angle on landing.

Club Uniforms and Equipment

In general fencing clubs are responsible for the equipment they provide being adequate and safe for anyone who uses it, especially for beginners. Maintaining club equipment is hard work and must be done on a regular schedule:

- weapons – your weapons must be kept in good condition with even bends in the blade, guards in their original shape with no deformation, coverings of the grip intact (not frayed, unraveling, or disintegrating), and buttons or electric tips in good condition on the point of the weapon. Blades should be sanded with a medium to fine grain sandpaper to remove nicks that could cause stress, to eliminate steel splinters, and to prevent corrosion forming. This can be made into an end of class duty – students sand their weapons before returning them to the weapons rack.

- masks – inspect all masks monthly and document your inspection. Minor corrosion may be removable using sand paper or steel wool, minor damage to bibs may be repaired, elastic straps can be replaced, and small dents can be gently hammered out with a ball-peen hammer. However, until these things are done by the armorer the mask should not be in service. Major damage means the mask should be immediately either discarded or retired to the head of a practice dummy.

    - A special note about masks with clear visors – every fencer who uses a lexan or other clear mask should read and heed the Federation Internationale d'Escrime's report on the lexan mask penetration in 2010 (FIE Urgent Letter 3 08-02-2010). Care of these masks must follow exactly the manufacturer's instruction. Failure to do so risks mask penetration.

- jackets – jackets need to be washed after use, period. Allowing sweat to stay in the cloth weakens threads, and letting dirt particles stay in the cloth can actually result in strands of fiber being cut. A dirty, yellowed, jacket that you can smell from the on guard line is disgusting, sends a horrible image of your club to beginners, and is unsafe. Minor tears and points of wear should be immediately patched – until they are the jacket should not be in service.

- gloves – most beginner level gloves now are washable. The comments above about jackets are just as true of gloves. Holes in the leather part of a glove mean replacement. Recent accidents (and the public warnings by the Federation Internationale d'Escrime about these events) involving the penetration of the finger webbing of gloves by sabres means that regular inspection of student gloves is important (FIE Information Letter 4 7-03-2011).

- plastrons (underarm protectors) – there have been enough accidents that involve penetrating injuries in arm pits to make plastron wear mandatory whenever fencers are going to fence each other. The same rules that apply to jackets apply to plastrons.

The bottom line – never handle a piece of club equipment without looking at it. If there is a problem do not give that uniform item or piece of equipment to a student to use. And discard what needs to be discarded – a new $12 glove or a new $45.00 mask is much cheaper than a trip to the emergency room for a penetrating injury.

23. Basic Fencing Records

Your salle, club, or team may already have standard forms used for a variety of purposes, including membership, medical and health, training conducted, equipment maintenance, etc. If you have you have records you should also have policies about how these records are processed and stored to meet legal and other requirements. Work with your professional coach so that you understand the use of the records, the policies that govern them, and which parts of the records fall in your area of responsibility. If your club does not keep records, you must maintain some basic records to help you develop your instructional skills and to protect you from liability. As a minimum, these records should be maintained for the period established by law during which you may be vulnerable to litigation.

Basic Personal Records

As a minimum you need to know:

- who you taught
- on what date
- what techniques and tactics you taught
- areas for follow-up in future lessons
- and if there were any unusual events, accidents, etc.

Your written lesson plans are probably the best way of recording this information. Date them, list the students in the class, make notations about follow-up needed, note any incidents, and save them in a file box (eventually a file cabinet). If you don't keep written lesson plans (even of the mini-type described above), as an absolute minimum keep an instructor log that records the same basic information. This does not have to be fancy, a bound record book with entries handwritten at the time in ink, is quite adequate. These become contemporaneous records that help establish in legally accepted ways:

- that you have used good judgment and adhered to commonly accepted practices in preparing your athletes – in case of litigation coming from injury, from an upset fencer or parent who believes that your training was inadequate, or from a variety of other reasons.

- who was present in the club. This is absolutely critical to defending yourself if there is ever a question about your conduct, in any litigation involving an injury, accident or sexual misconduct, if one of your students (especially one who is a child) is reported missing, etc.

- that you are teaching students professionally. This is essential to answer tax questions if you are receiving pay to teach and are charging expenses as business expenses. A lack of records indicates to tax auditors that what you are doing is a hobby, not employment or a business, with the potential for tax liability.

Accident Reports

If there is an accident on the premises where you teach in which you are involved in any way and that requires more than a band aid or a cold pack for a bruise, you must document it. As soon as possible after the accident write a basic report that records the answers to the following questions:

- what happened, including the condition of the injured athlete,
- when it happened, including date, time, and whether part of scheduled club activity,

- where it happened, the venue, where within the venue, and the condition of that space,
- who it happened to, and who else was there as possible witnesses, and
- how it happened – a short narrative of the event and the steps you took to respond to it.

Make a copy for your organization and retain the original. The basic principle of accident reports is to save accident reports forever. Statutes of limitations on personal injury vary from state to state, and may run from when the effects of the injury were discovered, not from the date of the injury.

Equipment Maintenance

In the case of an accident a standard question in any sport is whether the equipment used in the sport and involved in the accident was properly maintained. Failure to do so may be evidence of negligence, and has the potential to greatly increase your liability. Your club can limit its liability by having detailed written procedures for maintaining equipment and by demonstrating that those procedures are followed through maintenance records. If the club has an armorer, this is logically a duty of that position.

However, as a coach, you may be the only person interested in the condition of the equipment. As a minimum you should document any time you inspect or repair equipment. This can be as simple as a log book in which you record the date, piece of equipment, and the work done. Some of the items you should record include:

- monthly mask inspections, major cleaning, and punch tests,
- weapon repairs including grip, new blade, or guard replacements,
- weapons testing,
- jacket inspections and repairs,
- body cord testing and servicing, including cleaning, and
- servicing and repair of scoring equipment and electric strips.

Maintenance records should be retained permanently. Not only does this address the statute of limitations problem, but it also demonstrates that good maintenance practices are not a new thing, but rather a well-established practice, in case of litigation.

Tax Records

As an Assistant Moniteur you are not getting rich teaching fencing. However, the money that you receive for teaching is income, and the money you spend is expense. Income is taxable at the state and federal level; expense helps reduce your tax burden. Both need to be documented. As a minimum:

- talk to your tax preparer and understand what you need to report and how that should be recorded. Sometimes what you call an item in your records can make a difference as to whether it is deductible and whether it will raise the interest of an auditor.

- keep a simple ledger that indicates date, amount, from whom, and for what for each payment to you. You can do this with accounting software, but, unless you are working with a lot of payments, a ledger will work and will be significantly simpler.

- do the same for all expenses.

- save receipts for every expense. Make sure the receipt has a clear date, and if the purpose of the item is not completely obvious make a note on the receipt. As a general rule, it is cleaner if you do not mix business expenses and personal ones on the same receipt.

Do not try to do this on the basis that students slip you cash and you do not report it. First, you are violating the law, both state and federal. Second, there are severe penalties for doing so, both state and federal. Third, if a disgruntled student reports you, everything you do will get audited, not just your fencing income, and that is both time consuming and an opportunity for even more tax liability to be discovered. If you intend to be a professional, you have to operate as a professional and that includes paying taxes on your income.

Improving Performance

Your personal teaching records are potentially a gold mine of information that reflects how your teaching evolves. This information is critical to your development as a coach and your future plans to qualify as a Moniteur, Prevot, or Maitre. Records of your lessons are a living tool, not something to be dropped in a file box and forgotten. They can help you plan how to make your students more successful, but they also provide you a guide to improving your coaching.

The first step is to make notes on every lesson you teach. These do not have to be long or elaborate, but they should be distinctive enough that you can easily identify the areas for work. Include items such as:

- what worked and what did not work – content, demonstrations, drills, timing,
- common student problems and how you fixed them, and
- areas in your teaching or fencing technique in which you need to seek more training.

Review these regularly. I do a week to week review before I teach the next week's session. When I finish a specific course, such as our beginner's class, I review the notes for the entire class. Other obvious times are at the end of a training cycle, such as the microcycles, mesoycles, and macrocycles of the annual periodized training program (if you are not familiar with periodized training, it will be discussed in a future handbook of this series).

APPENDIX 1– How this Handbook Addresses the National Standards for Sports Coaches

The National Association for Sport and Physical Education published the 2nd edition of *Quality Coaches, Quality Sports: National Standards for Sport Coaches*, in 2006. This document, adopted by over 100 sports organizations, ranging from local to national, provides the only national view of appropriate standards for coaches in all sports. As might be expected in a reference for entry level coaches, this handbook does not fully address all of the standards and their associated benchmarks. However, I have listed the standards below, and indicated which sections provide the reader with information that will help you work toward fully meeting the National Standards, both in the intent of your practice and the content of your fencing program. I strongly recommend that you purchase and use the *National Standards* as a basic coaching reference.

Domain and Standard	Addressed in Section
1 – Philosophy and Ethics	
Standard 1 – Develop and implement an athlete-centered coaching philosophy	1, 2, 4, 6
Standard 2 – Identify, model, and teach positive values learned through sport participation	4, 6
Standard 3 – Teach and reinforce responsible personal, social, and ethical behavior of all people involved in the sport program	4, 6, 18, 19
Standard 4 – Demonstrate ethical conduct in all facets of the sport program	4, 5, 6, 18, 19
2 – Safety and Injury Prevention	
Standard 5 – Prevent injuries by providing safe facilities	7
Standard 6 – Ensure that all necessary protective equipment is available, properly fitted, and used appropriately	7, 22
Standard 7 – Monitor environmental conditions and modify participation as needed to ensure the health and safety of participants	7
Standard 8 – Identify physical conditions that predispose athletes to injuries	Not addressed
Standard 9 – Recognize injuries and provide immediate and appropriate care	7
Standard 10 – Facilitate a coordinated sports health care program that includes prevention, care, and management of injuries	Not addressed
Standard 11 – Identify and address the psychological implications of injury	Not addressed
3 – Physical Conditioning	
Standard 12 – Design programs of training, conditioning, and recovery that properly utilize exercise physiology and biomechanical principles	16, 17
Standard 13 – Teach and encourage proper nutrition for optimal physical and mental performance and overall good health	Not addressed
Standard 14 – Be an advocate for drug-free sport participation and provide accurate information about drugs and supplements	4
Standard 15 – Plan conditioning programs to help athletes return to full participation following injury.	Not addressed
4 – Growth and Development	

Standard 16 – Apply knowledge of how developmental change influences the learning and performance of sport skills	Not addressed
Standard 17 – Facilitate the social and emotional growth of athletes by supporting a positive sports experience and lifelong participation in physical activity	Not addressed
Standard 18 – Provide athletes with responsibility and leadership opportunities as they mature	Introduction, 2
5 – Teaching and Communication	
Standard 19 – Provide a positive learning environment that is appropriate to the characteristics of the athlete and goals of the program	6, 16, 17
Standard 20 – Develop and monitor goals for the athletes and program	Not addressed
Standard 21 – Organize practice based on a seasonal or annual practice plan to maintain motivation, manage fatigue, and allow for peak performance at the appropriate time	Not addressed
Standard 22 – Plan and implement daily practice activities that maximize time on task and available resources	14, 15, 16, 17
Standard 23 – Utilize appropriate instructional strategies to facilitate athlete development and performance	13, 14, 15, 16, 17
Standard 24 – Teach and incorporate mental skills to enhance performance and reduce sport anxiety.	Not addressed
Standard 25 – Use effective communications skills to enhance individual learning, group success, and enjoyment in the sport experience	12, 14, 16, 17
Standard 26 – Demonstrate and utilize appropriate and effective motivational techniques to enhance athlete performance and satisfaction	Not addressed
6 – Sports Skills and Tactics	
Standard 27 – Know the skills, elements of skill combinations, and techniques associated with the sport being coached	12, 14
Standard 28 – Identify, develop, and apply competitive sport strategies and specific tactics appropriate for the age and skill levels of the participating athletes	10, 11, 12, 14
Standard 29 – Use scouting methods for planning practices, game preparation, and game analysis	Not addressed
7 – Organization and Administration	
Standard 30 – Demonstrate efficiency in contest management	Not addressed
Standard 31 – Be involved in public relation activities for the sport program	Not addressed
Standard 32 – Manage human resources for the program	5
Standard 33 – Manage fiscal resources for the program	23
Standard 34 – Facilitate planning, implementation, and documentation of the emergency action plan	7, 22, 23
Standard 35 – Manage all information, documents, and records for the program	16, 23
Standard 36 – Fulfill all legal responsibilities and risk management procedures associated with coaching	1, 2, 4, 5, 6, 7, 22, 23

8 – Evaluation	
Standard 37 – Implement effective evaluation techniques for team performance in relation to established goals	21, 23
Standard 38 – Use a variety of strategies to evaluate athlete motivation and individual performance as they relate to season objectives and goals	21
Standard 39 – Utilize an effective and objective process for evaluation of athletes in order to assign roles or positions and establish individual goals	21
Standard 40 – Utilize an objective and effective process for evaluation of self and staff	Not addressed

APPENDIX 2 – A First Library for Professional Coaches

As Assistant Moniteurs it is time to start to develop a professional library of fencing textbooks. There are a wide variety of current and almost current texts that provide a solid knowledge base for the sport. We suggest the following as first books to buy:

Foil:
Paul Sise, *A Basic Foil Companion**
Istvan Lukovich , *Electric Foil Fencing*

Epee:
Johan Harmenberg, *Epee 2.0: the Birth of the New Fencing Paradigm**
Imre Vass, *Epee Fencing: A Complete System**

Sabre:
Zbigniew Borysiuk, *Modern Saber Fencing: Technique, Tactics, Training, Research**
Rob Handelman, *Fencing: A Practical Guide for Training Young Athletes*

Sports Psychology:
Aladar Kogler, *One Touch at a Time**

The Rules:
USA Fencing, *Fencing Rules*, current edition
USA Fencing, *Athlete Handbook*, current edition

Coaching:
The National Association for Sport and Physical Education, *Quality Coaches, Quality Sports: National Standards for Sport Coaches*, 2nd edition

Books with an asterisk are available from SK Swordplay Books at http://swordplaybooks.com.

Rob Handelman's book is available from San Francisco Youth Sports at their website at http://www.sfyouthfencing.com/Fencing_Book_Order.html.

Istvan Lukovich's book is out of print, but copies may be found at various fencing vendors, and a new edition is reported to be in the works.

The two USA Fencing publications are available as .pdf files under the Resources – Documents pull down on USA Fencing's website at http://usfencing.org.

Quality Coaches, Quality Sports: National Standards for Sport Coaches can be ordered from the American Alliance for Health, Physical Education, Recreation and Dance at www.aahperd.org/naspe.

APPENDIX 3 – Assignments to Start to Prepare for the Moniteur Examination

As you qualify as an Asssistant Moniteur, we encourage you to continue your development as a coach. In preparation for the first Moniteur Workshop in the National Training Program, I suggest the following steps:

1. Improve your personal technique in the following skills. Concentrate on clean, modern, standard performance of the skill, and avoid personal interpretations which work for you, but which do not translate to students:

    - Positions of attention and on guard
    - Salute
    - Advance
    - Retreat
    - Lunge
    - Advance lunge
    - Straight thrust (in foil and epee, in sabre cuts to the head, flank, and chest)
    - Disengage (in foil and epee)
    - Change of engagement (in foil)
    - Counterdisengage (in foil and epee)
    - Coupe (in sabre)
    - Parries 4th and 6th (6th and circular 6th in epee, 3rd, 4th, and 5th in sabre)
    - Direct riposte
    - Coupe (in foil)
    - Disengage point thrust (in sabre)
    - Feint straight thrust-disengage
    - Feint straight thrust-counterdisengage
    - One-two
    - Double
    - Stop Hit

2. Assist in teaching as many group lessons as possible. As a minimum:

    - Lead warm-ups at least a dozen times.
    - Lead drills at least 30 times.
    - Teach at least 30 short assessment or check lessons.
    - Demonstrate every skill listed above for your weapon, preferably several times.
    - Do at least a dozen lesson plans and use them to teach a technique from the list above.

Index

Because this handbook contains a wide variety of material, some of which is referenced in a number of locations, it seemed important to include a reasonably detailed index to help the reader locate specific topics. Any index is always a compromise in terms of the amount of detail, and is a reflection of how the author views the subject matter. Hopefully this index will be useful when you absolutely have to find a definition, concept, technique, or tactic.

Made in the USA
Columbia, SC
25 May 2025

58430728R00050